DYSLEXIA: HOW TO SURVIVE AND SUCCEED AT WORK

Also by this author:
Dyslexia: A Teenager's Guide (Vermilion, 2004)

Dyslexia:

How to survive and succeed at work

DR SYLVIA MOODY

Vermilion
LONDON

1 3 5 7 9 10 8 6 4 2

First published in the United Kingdom in 2006 by Vermilion, an imprint of Ebury Publishing Random House UK Ltd. Random House 20 Vauxhall Bridge Road London SW1V 2SA

Random House Australia (Pty) Limited 20 Alfred Street, Milsons Point, Sydney, New South Wales 2061, Australia

Random House New Zealand Limited 18 Poland Road, Glenfield, Auckland 10, New Zealand

Random House (Pty) Limited Isle of Houghton, Corner of Boundary Road & Carse O'Gowrie, Houghton 2198, South Africa

Random House Publishers India Private Limited 301 World Trade Tower, Hotel Intercontinental Grand Complex, Barakhamba Lane, New Delhi 110 001, India

Random House UK Limited Reg. No. 954009 www.randomhouse.co.uk Papers used by Vermilion are natural, recyclable products made from wood grown in sustainable forests. A CIP catalogue record is available for this book from the British Library.

ISBN: 009190708X ISBN 13: 9780091907082 (from January 2007)

Typeset by SX Composing DTP, Rayleigh, Essex

Printed and bound in Great Britain by Mackays of Chatham plc, Chatham, Kent

Copies are available at special rates for bulk orders. Contact the sales development team on 020 7840 8487 or visit www.booksforpromotions.co.uk for more information.

Contents

Acknowledgements

In writing this book I have greatly benefited from the advice and support of my colleagues:

Diana Bartlett
Susan Close
Katherine Kindersley

I should also like to thank my clients, James, Laura, Gina and Krishnan, for allowing me to transcribe conversations we have had together.

Preface

A note to my reader.

I assume you are a person who either has – or is seeking – a job, and I would like to ask you the following questions.

Do you consider yourself, as a working person, to be a model of efficiency, the envy of your colleagues and the darling of your managers? Or would you just say you get by reasonably well in an average sort of way? Or do you feel that your working day is a nightmare of inefficiency, anxiety and frustration?

If the last statement is true, do you know why? Is it because you are lazy, unmotivated and incompetent? Or is it rather the case that you feel you have some good abilities, but that these are constantly undermined by baffling inefficiencies? However hard you try, however many hours you put in, your work does not come up to scratch. If this is the case, have you ever considered whether you might be dyslexic?

Dyslexia is a syndrome of difficulties that is well recognised in the educational sphere, but awareness of it in the workplace is partial and patchy. This book is an attempt to remedy that situation.

In the first section of this book I'll explain in detail what dyslexic difficulties are, and how they cause problems in the workplace. I shall also describe a related set of difficulties called dyspraxia. I'll then explain how to go about getting an assessment for these two types of difficulty.

In the second part of the book, I'll suggest strategies that you yourself can use to manage your difficulties, capitalise on your strengths and improve your efficiency at work.

The third part of the book gives information about ways in which employers can offer help and support, and explains how the Disability Discrimination Act 1995 applies to dyslexia and dyspraxia.

I hope that you – and your employer – will find this book helpful, and that it will enable you to get a fuller understanding of your difficulties and how to overcome them.

Dr Sylvia Moody
Dyslexia Assessment Service
London

PART A

DYSLEXIA OBSERVED

In this first section of the book, I'll explain the nature of dyslexic difficulties and describe how these affect efficiency in working life. I'll also discuss the related syndrome of dyspraxia. Finally, I'll give advice on how to arrange an assessment and what you should expect to gain from the assessment process.

CHAPTER 1

WHAT IS DYSLEXIA?

It might seem obvious that a book on dyslexia should begin with a definition of the term 'dyslexia'. But, alas, this is not possible, because there is at present no agreement among experts on exactly how dyslexia should be defined, or what might be its cause. As the saying goes: two experts, three opinions.

Some researchers adopt a 'narrow' definition of dyslexia: they view it simply as a difficulty with word reading (*dyslexia* means literally 'difficulty with words'), and they search for the cause of this. Other researchers adopt a wider definition. They view dyslexia as a syndrome, or group, of difficulties that includes problems with literacy skills, memory, perception, sequencing and organisational skills. Researchers who take this view tend to be less concerned with the cause of dyslexia and more interested in its effects.

DYSLEXIA AS A SYNDROME

In this book, I shall adopt this wider view of dyslexia as a syndrome of difficulties, and shall be particularly concerned with how these difficulties affect efficiency in working life. To put some 'flesh' on this syndrome, I present below the experience of a dyslexic client of mine, James, who holds an administrative post in a large organisation.

When James first consulted me, he had no idea that he might be dyslexic. All he knew was that he was experiencing difficulties at work, and that his job was under threat. He described his situation as follows:

> In many ways I enjoy my work, and I have the right qualifications for it. But from day to day I seem to get a lot of things wrong. Mainly, it's just silly mistakes. I'll get a telephone number down wrongly, or mis-read something, or make spelling mistakes with simple words. It baffles me how these things happen, because I do check my work. I just don't seem to see the mistakes.
>
> Another thing is that I'm quite disorganised. I tend to forget appointments, and when I'm told anything, it seems to go in one ear and out of the other. I'm constantly losing things or filing them in the wrong place. I think one problem is that I feel rushed and stressed all the time. The office is quite noisy and busy and I find it hard to concentrate on what I'm doing. I keep changing from one task to another and tend to lose track of what's urgent and what's not.
>
> I often stay late at the office or take work home in order to get something finished, and I can get really

exhausted with it all. So it annoys me when my manager makes remarks implying that I'm lazy or not conscientious. I don't know why I'm so inefficient – I feel really stupid sometimes and wonder if I should look for a less demanding job.

Clearly, James was not only irritated by his inefficiencies, but also completely baffled by them. As an intelligent, hard-working and conscientious person, he found it hard to understand why he was always making mistakes and forgetting things.

And it was not only James who felt baffled. His line manager was similarly at a loss to understand his behaviour. In her work review report on James, she noted that:

James has many strengths: he is intelligent and imaginative, and good at problem solving. He is an excellent strategic thinker. However, on a day-to-day basis, he is very careless in his work, and seems to have no concept of deadlines or work schedules. His timekeeping is poor, and he often comes in late, claiming that he has overslept. He seems to make no attempt to improve his work, and in discussions I have had with him about the situation, he has been either offhand and flippant, or surly and defensive. Unless he can improve his work and his attitude, his long-term future with the company must be in doubt.

OPPOSING VIEWPOINTS

It is clear from the above that, while James and his line manager both recognised that there were problems, they saw James's attitude to them rather differently. James was annoyed with himself for making mistakes, did his best to correct them, and worked overtime in order to get things finished. In fact he was wearing himself out trying to get his job done properly.

By contrast, his line manager saw him as lazy, slapdash and unco-operative. She tended to view him as being difficult rather than as having difficulties. In consequence, James felt offended and misunderstood. Dialogue between him and his manager broke down.

DYSLEXIA AND RELATIONSHIPS

Nor was it just at work that communication became difficult. Problems also arose at home. When James came for his first meeting with me, he was accompanied by his wife, Laura. It was Laura who had first suspected that James might be dyslexic, but when she tried to discuss this with him he had dismissed the idea, saying he couldn't be dyslexic because he enjoyed reading. Laura described her own feelings about the situation as follows:

> James and I used to be very close – we'd always discuss everything together and sort out any problems. But recently it seems as if there's some barrier between us. I know he has problems at work, but he refuses to talk about them. I get the impression he thinks he's some sort

of failure – he just mopes around the house all the time and seems to have lost interest in everything. He's completely shut me out.

Everything about the above scenario inclined me to the opinion that James might well be dyslexic. He was obviously an intelligent and able person in many ways, but was inefficient in office tasks that depended on literacy skills, memory and organisational ability. The fact that he *was* generally such an able person meant that he felt frustrated and angry with himself when he was inefficient, and became quite 'prickly' when other people remarked on his inefficiency. He felt that he ought to be able to sort out the problems himself by putting in more effort and working longer hours. When this didn't work, he became despondent and retreated more and more into himself, shutting out both his work colleagues and his family.

My formal assessment of James confirmed that the pattern of his abilities and difficulties was typical of that found in the profile of dyslexic adults. He had good reasoning ability, an adequate vocabulary and good general knowledge. His reading was slow, but reasonably competent. He scored badly on tests of spelling, memory, perception and sequencing skills.

Both James and Laura were relieved to find that James had a well-recognised set of difficulties, for which he could now be given effective help. Following the assessment, James began a training programme with a specialist dyslexic tutor, and his employer, as required by law, took appropriate measures in the workplace to help and support him. In a relatively brief period of time, James was able to improve his skills, and to make more effective use of his many strengths. As a result, he became less stressed and his relations with those around him became easier. His job is no longer under threat.

A WIDESPREAD PROBLEM

Dyslexic difficulties create problems not just for office workers, but for people in a wide variety of jobs. For example, a lorry driver has to fill in timesheets, an actor has to remember lines, a carpenter needs to be accurate with measurements.

Whatever your job, if you feel that you have difficulties at work that are similar to those described in this chapter, complete the following checklist to see if your difficulties match a typical dyslexia profile.

Workplace Dyslexia Checklist

Tick the items that cause you difficulty:

READING
Following written instructions ❑
Following technical manuals ❑
Quickly getting the gist of letters/reports, etc ❑
Recalling what you have read ❑

WRITING
Writing reversible letters (b and d) ❑
Sequencing letters (which – wihch) ❑
Spelling ❑

Grammar ❑

Punctuation ❑

Handwriting ❑

Filling in forms ❑

Expressing ideas clearly in writing ❑

Writing memos/letters ❑

Writing reports ❑

Taking notes/minutes ❑

NUMERICAL DATA

Copying numbers ❑

Putting numbers in columns/tables ❑

Doing arithmetical calculations ❑

SPEECH AND COMPREHENSION

Following a conversation/discussion ❑

Contributing to a discussion/meeting ❑

Presenting your thoughts clearly ❑

MEMORY AND CONCENTRATION

Following oral instructions ❑

Remembering:

       telephone numbers ❑

       messages ❑

       appointments ❑

Concentrating for long periods ❑

VISUO-MOTOR SKILLS

Inputting data on a computer/calculator ❑

Analysing complex visual arrays (tables of figures, graphs) ❑

Getting your bearings in large or complex buildings ❑

SEQUENCING

Filing ❏

Retrieving files ❏

Looking up entries in dictionaries/directories ❏

ORGANISATION

Planning work schedules ❏

Meeting deadlines ❏

Keeping papers in order ❏

Working efficiently ❏

KEY TIPS

- Understanding the nature of your difficulties is the first step towards managing them.
- Dyslexia is not just about reading – you could be a reasonably fluent reader and still have dyslexic difficulties.

CHAPTER 2

DYSLEXIA AT WORK

Reading through the account of dyslexic difficulties in the previous chapter, you might have felt bewildered by the amount and range of them. How does slow reading relate to forgetting instructions? How does poor spelling relate to being disorganised? And is there any aspect of work that *isn't* affected by dyslexia?

Dyslexic difficulties can be grouped into three main categories, and each category of difficulty affects work in different ways. The three categories of dyslexia are:

- Auditory dyslexia
- Visual dyslexia
- Processing speed dyslexia

These terms are explained below. But, first, it is important to stress that these three types of dyslexia are rarely found in a 'pure' form. Most people have a mixture of all three. So when we say, for example, that someone is an 'auditory dyslexic', we usually mean that their difficulties are *mainly* auditory, not wholly so.

AUDITORY DYSLEXIA

The word 'auditory' means 'connected with hearing'. But auditory dyslexia is not a problem with hearing itself; rather it is a problem with remembering what is heard. In other words, it denotes a weakness in *auditory memory*.

How does auditory memory work?

There are two types of auditory memory: *long-term memory* and *short-term memory*.

- Long-term memory is used for remembering things on a more or less permanent basis – for example, the words of a poem we learnt as a child, and can still remember.
- Short-term memory is used for remembering things for a limited period, perhaps just for a few seconds – for example, remembering a telephone number, or some instructions we have just been given. Here are two short-term memory tasks for you to try:

Task 1. Read through the following list of words ONCE only, and then try to remember them *without glancing back* at the list:

lion, apple, table, snow, knife, light, coat, paper, hammer

Task 2. Read through the following sum ONCE only, and then try to work out the answer *in your head*.

Add 8 and 4, divide by 2, and multiply by 5
(The answer is given at the end of the chapter.)

If you are dyslexic, you may have a particular difficulty with these tasks, because, in auditory dyslexia, it is this *short-term* memory that is inefficient. And it can be inefficient in two ways. To understand this, we need to look in more detail at the workings of the memory system.

Look back at tasks 1 and 2 above, and you will see that they were slightly different. In task 1, you just had to *recall* some information. In task 2 you had to both *recall* information (the sum given to you) and at the same time *work on* the information, that is, work out the answer to the sum in your head.

In task 1, your memory was passive: it functioned simply as a *storage* memory. In task 2, your memory was active: it operated as a *working* memory.

In dyslexia, both the storage and working components of the memory system can be inefficient. The diagram below will help you to visualise how these components work together and what can go wrong.

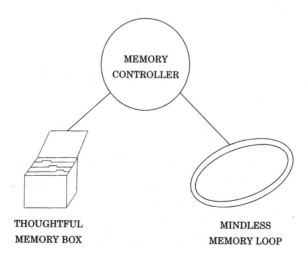

MEMORY
CONTROLLER

THOUGHTFUL
MEMORY BOX

MINDLESS
MEMORY LOOP

The *memory controller* at the centre of the system is the active working component of memory: it inspects any information coming into the memory system and works on it appropriately. It is helped in its work by two 'assistants': the *mindless memory loop* and the *thoughtful memory box*, both of which are storage systems.

The *loop* is like a fan belt – it has no brains and simply rotates at the command of the controller, mindlessly repeating information it is given. The *box*, however, is intelligent – it can store information it receives from the controller in a logical 'easy to find' way. It can also hold a greater amount of information than the loop, and can store it for a much longer period.

The following two examples will make clear how the *mindless memory loop* and the *thoughtful memory box* assist the *memory controller* in its work.

THE MINDLESS MEMORY LOOP

Look again at the mental arithmetic question I gave you above:

Add 8 and 4, divide by 2, and multiply by 5

When a complicated task like this comes into the memory system, the *controller* gets to work on it. But it can't handle all the calculations needed at the same time. While it is busy adding 8 and 4, it must ensure that it doesn't forget the rest of the sum. So it 'throws' the whole sum into the *memory loop*, and orders this to go round and round mindlessly repeating it. So now the *controller* can concentrate on adding 8 and 4. Then, as it gradually progresses along the sum, the *controller* takes back information as needed from the loop.

An important point to note about the *mindless memory loop* is that it has a very limited capacity. It could remember a sum like the one above, but if the sum became much longer, the loop would be overloaded and would break down. To avoid overload, the loop has to throw out old information as soon as new information comes in.

THE THOUGHTFUL MEMORY BOX

Imagine the following situation.

You are sitting on a bus thinking about a letter you are going to write as part of a job application. You have no writing materials about you, so you have to plan out the letter in your head. As you think through what you want to say, you have to keep in mind, at any given moment, everything that you have already said, so that you don't repeat yourself.

Your *memory controller* can't put all this information into the *mindless memory loop*, because that store is too limited and too short-term. On the other hand, the information doesn't need to be kept in your mind for ever, so it isn't appropriate to forward it to long-term memory. In the circumstances, the *thoughtful memory box* is the ideal location. It can hold a large amount of material, and because it is thoughtful, it will keep it in a logical order, thereby making it easy to find at a later date, when you actually sit down to write your letter.

Auditory memory and dyslexia

In dyslexia, then, something has gone wrong with this memory system. It may be that the loop and/or the box are faulty, or it might be that communication between the controller and its two memory assistants is disrupted in some way. Whatever the cause, the consequence can be inefficiency in any tasks that depend on short-term auditory memory.

Auditory memory and phonology

'Phonology' is a Greek word meaning 'the study of sound'. When we speak, write or listen, we have to process the sounds of our language. We have to be able to recognise sounds, assign the correct sounds to letters, and put sounds together in the correct order to make words. The technical name for this last skill is 'phonological sequencing ability'. And this is an ability that depends heavily upon auditory short-term memory. When you are in the process of saying a long word, you have to remember, as you go along, which bits of the word you have already said. For this, you rely on your *mindless memory loop*.

If you are dyslexic, you may have some difficulty with this. You may find that you miss out parts of words, or get letters in the wrong order. So, for example, you might say *conversation* for *conservation*, *irrisible* for *irresistible*, *pneunomia* for *pneumonia*. What has happened here is that the word has got so long that your *memory loop* has 'crashed'. And this same difficulty arises, not just in speech, but also when you are writing or hearing long words.

Auditory memory at work

Poor auditory memory causes a number of difficulties in the workplace, and these can be grouped according to which part of the memory system is inefficient.

As explained above, one component of your memory storage system is the *mindless memory loop*. If this is not working efficiently, expect to have difficulty with:

- Writing down telephone numbers
- Writing down figures
- Writing down dates
- Remembering names when you are introduced to people
- Writing down people's names when they spell them out to you

If you do have these problems, then you are likely to make mistakes when you have to take down information over the telephone from clients or colleagues.

The second component of your memory storage system is the *thoughtful memory box*. If this is inefficient, expect to have difficulties with:

- Understanding the meaning of what you read
- Getting your thoughts in a logical order when writing or speaking
- Thinking about things in a focused way

- Explaining things clearly to people
- Following the gist of conversations and discussions
- Taking notes

If you experience these problems, you will find that you are slow in any task involving literacy skills, and you may have difficulty contributing to work discussions and meetings.

As noted above, weak auditory memory is associated with poor *phonological sequencing* ability. This can cause you problems with:

- Saying and writing long names or words
- Reading words accurately
- Spelling regular words

But it's not just phonological sequencing that is affected. Poor memory makes *any sort of sequencing* difficult. So it could cause problems with:

- Remembering instructions
- Giving instructions to other people
- Doing a sequence of tasks in the correct order
- Organising your work schedule

Clearly, auditory memory has its 'tentacles' everywhere – it affects just about everything you might do in a working day. However, the good news is that there are many ways to compensate for poor memory, and we shall be looking at relevant strategies in Section B of this book.

VISUAL DYSLEXIA

There are two problem areas in visual dyslexia: *visual perception* and *visual memory*.

Visual perception

This is a combination of the eye seeing something, and the brain making sense of what the eye sees. So, for example, if your eye sees this:

H

your brain would interpret the shape according to the context in which it appears.

One context could be:

Harry

so the brain would see the shape as a capital letter H.

Another context could be:

So now the brain would see the shape as part of a ladder.

Visual memory

Short-term memory works in much the same way as auditory short-term memory. The chief difference is that, instead of a mindless memory *loop*, you have a mindless memory *screen*. Images of everything you see appear on the screen for a second or two before fading.

Visual dyslexia at work

If your *visual perception* is poor, expect to have difficulties with:

- Spotting mistakes in written work
- Looking up entries in dictionaries or directories
- Filing
- Dealing with complex tables of data
- Doing written sums
- Reading through lists
- Scanning through text
- Following flow charts
- Looking at words or numbers on a computer screen
- Reading measurements

If your *visual memory* is poor, you may find it hard to:

- Remember spellings, especially of irregular words
- Remember spellings you've just looked up in the dictionary
- Recall where you've put, or filed, things
- Remember whereabouts in a book or report you read something

- Recall plans or diagrams
- Find your way about in large buildings
- Find your way from one place to another in the outside world

Again, be assured that, in the second part of this book, you will be learning plenty of strategies to deal with these difficulties.

PROCESSING SPEED DYSLEXIA

A general difficulty reported by most dyslexic people is slowness in processing information. Usually this difficulty is found in combination with one or both of the other two types of dyslexia described above: auditory and visual. However, it can sometimes occur independently of any obvious visual or auditory problems, and can therefore be more difficult to spot. It manifests itself chiefly as a general slowness in working on any task, but particularly in reading and writing.

DYSLEXIA AT WORK:
PROBLEMS AND SOLUTIONS

'Reading lessons in church is my nightmare. I tend to lose my place in the passage I'm reading. So I've cut out a little reading window in a piece of cardboard and I track down the page with this.' *Judith, vicar*

'I find using the kiln difficult. I tend to make mistakes with the timing and the temperature gauges. I find it

helps to use a magnifying glass to look at the gauges, and I say the numbers out loud as I read them.' *Simon, potter*

'I'm very forgetful and have a bad habit of going off to work without things I need, such as binoculars or my notebook. Now I've tacked up a list by the front door of everything I could possibly need during the day. So far I haven't forgotten to check the list!' *Jenny, National Trust warden*

VISUAL STRESS

Before leaving this review of dyslexic difficulties, I want to mention a syndrome called 'visual stress', which, though not specifically a dyslexic difficulty, is often associated with dyslexia.

Sufferers from visual stress report that they see print 'swimming about on the page', and that white paper seems to 'glare'. They find bright light, especially fluorescent lighting, disturbing, and tend to develop headaches when reading for any length of time.

These symptoms are not usually picked up in a standard eye test, so if you think you might have visual stress, you may wish to arrange an assessment with an optometrist who specialises in colorimetry. As an interim 'do-it-yourself' measure, you could purchase inexpensive coloured overlays or eye-level reading rulers. (See pages 188–189 for more details of sources of help.) Opposite is a visual stress checklist.

Do You Have Visual Stress?

Tick any items that apply to you.

1 Do you find it hard to focus on written text? ❑

2 Does reading make you tired? ❑

3 Do you often lose your place when reading? ❑

4 Do you re-read or skip lines when reading? ❑

5 Do you ever read words/numbers back to front? ❑

6 Do you miss out words when reading? ❑

7 Do you tend to misread words? ❑

8 Do you use a marker or your finger to keep your place? ❑

9 Are you easily distracted when reading? ❑

10 Do you become restless or fidgety when reading? ❑

11 Do you get headaches when you read? ❑

12 Do your eyes become sore or water? ❑

13 Do you screw your eyes up when reading? ❑

14 Do you rub or close one eye when reading? ❑

15 Do you read close to the page? ❑

16 Do you push the page away? ❑

17 Do you prefer dim light to bright light for reading? ❑

18 Does white paper (or white board) seem to glare? ❑

19 Does it all become harder the longer you read? ❑

20 Does print become distorted as you read? ❑

© Melanie Jameson

DO YOU HAVE A PROBLEM?

If you have already been diagnosed as dyslexic, you will no doubt be familiar with many of the difficulties described in this chapter. However, it may be that you are just wondering if you are dyslexic, and thinking that one or more of the dyslexic syndromes described above seem to fit with difficulties you are experiencing. Perhaps you have completed the Workplace Dyslexia checklist in Chapter 1, and found that you ticked many of the boxes.

Here now is a further checklist – on everyday dyslexic difficulties. If, again, you tick a lot of the boxes, then it might be time to start thinking of having a formal assessment.

Everyday Dyslexic Difficulties

Tick any items that cause you difficulty.

Writing a cheque	❑
Filling in forms	❑
Writing letters	❑
Reading letters	❑
Reading official documents	❑
Reading a newspaper	❑
Understanding operating/safety instructions on household gadgets	❑
Reading television schedules	❑
Reading recipes	❑
Reading bus/train timetables	❑
Making shopping lists	❑
Dealing with money in shops	❑
Checking bank statements	❑
Keeping track of outstanding bills	❑
Explaining things clearly to others	❑

Placing orders over the telephone ❑

Conducting enquiries over the telephone ❑

Following spoken instructions ❑

Following left–right instructions ❑

Reading maps ❑

Reading signposts ❑

Orienting yourself in a strange place or complex
  environment (e.g. tube station) ❑

Remembering where things have been put ❑

Looking up telephone numbers in directories ❑

Recording telephone numbers correctly ❑

Remembering messages ❑

Remembering appointments ❑

Organising daily life ❑

Concentrating for longer than an hour ❑

[Answer to sum on page 12: 30]

KEY TIPS

- If you have ticked many of the items on the Everyday Difficulties checklist, consider having a formal dyslexia assessment.
- If text 'swims' on the page, or white paper seems to 'glare', you may be suffering from *visual stress*.
- *Coloured overlays* and *eye-level reading rulers* relieve visual stress, and you can get professional advice from an optometrist who specialises in colorimetry.

CHAPTER 3

DYSPRAXIA AT WORK

Having read through the last chapter, you may feel that you have a set of difficulties that seem similar to dyslexia, but which don't quite fit the profiles described above. You may, for example, have literacy and memory problems, but also difficulties with physical co-ordination and directional sense, and perhaps also with social skills. Difficulties of this type are often grouped together under the name 'dyspraxia'.

As was the case with dyslexia, different groups of experts employ different definitions of dyspraxia. In the medical world, dyspraxia is defined very precisely as difficulty with motor skills, i.e. difficulty with planning and executing movement. In the educational world, the term is usually taken in the broader sense of difficulty with both *spatial* and *motor skills*.

Many people have a mixture of dyspraxic and dyslexic difficulties and so all the information given in this book about dyslexia will also be relevant to people with dyspraxia.

SPATIAL SKILLS

'Spatial skills' means the ability to orient oneself in space, for example to find one's way around in a big building, or in a complex environment like a railway station. It means the ability to see the relation of parts to the whole; for instance, many people know particular areas in their city quite well, but are unable to say where any one of these areas is in relation to the others. Another spatial problem could be judging distance, for example judging how close you are to the kerb when parking a car.

Interestingly, these spatial problems can also cause problems in social life, because in our social relations with other people, we have to be aware of 'social space'. We have to judge the correct distance we should place ourselves from another person in order not to seem, on the one hand, too threatening, or, on the other hand, too disengaged. We have to judge how loudly or softly we should speak, according to the circumstances: a lover might frighten off his beloved if he bellowed out his endearments at a party; a lecturer would cause irritation if she spoke too softly.

Another important social skill is turn-taking in conversation. It may not be immediately obvious that this is a spatial skill, but in fact a conversation can usefully be thought of as a filler of social space. If one person hogs the whole space, crowding out the other person, then the conversation has really become a monologue. It's important for both parties in the conversation to negotiate the space between them to ensure that both do their share of talking and listening.

MOTOR SKILLS

'Motor skills' refers to physical co-ordination: the ability to plan and execute movements. There are two categories of motor skills:

- Fine motor skill, needed for performing small movements such as handwriting, threading a needle and using cutlery
- Gross motor skill, needed for performing large movements, such as playing sports, driving a car and stacking shelves

EVERYDAY DYSPRAXIC DIFFICULTIES

Dyspraxia can cause many problems in everyday life. A dyspraxic client of mine, Gina, who is a self-employed gardener, describes her difficulties as follows:

> I've always been a very clumsy person. I'm forever bumping into things and tripping over or twisting my ankle. I've usually got a bruise somewhere and can't remember how I got it. I often put my clothes on inside out and have difficulty with buttons and zips. I'm very

messy generally, embarrassingly so when I'm eating. And I can make a real mess of filling a flowerpot.

At school I wasn't very good at sports. I never learnt to dance either, or to ride a bike. I had about ten driving lessons, but then had to give up. I had enough problems working out what to do with my feet, let alone keeping an eye on what was going on outside the car.

I do have a tendency to day-dream and I'm easily distracted. I often lose the thread of a conversation or I interrupt people so I don't forget what I'm about to say. I can get tongue-tied and trip over my words in meetings or on the 'phone. I can't easily explain things to people even though I understand them perfectly well myself. All this makes social life a bit difficult, and I don't find it very easy to make friends with people.

Gina was obviously annoyed and frustrated by her difficulties, but, as we shall see later in the book (Chapter 9), she was able to find ways to deal positively with them.

DYSPRAXIA IN THE WORKPLACE

Dyspraxia causes numerous problems in the workplace, both practical and social.

Problems with physical tasks

Physical clumsiness causes problems for people who work in manual trades, particularly if, like decorators or telephone engineers, they are required to do very careful work. But even office workers could have difficulty with some aspects of their work, for example:

- Typing
- Writing
- Keying in numbers on a telephone or calculator
- Using a date stamp
- Using a photocopier or other equipment
- Carrying files or books
- Carrying trays with coffee mugs

Problems with spatial tasks

If you have a job which involves travel, there are several difficulties you could encounter. You might find it difficult to read maps, and to find your way around in unfamiliar places. You could lose your bearings in airports or large railway stations. And you could have difficulty reading bus and train timetables.

Even if you just commute to and from the office every day, you could find yourself in difficulty if, for any reason, you could not take your usual route. A traffic diversion, a closed tube station, a last-minute change of platform for your train – all these could leave you floundering.

If you work in a large office building, you might easily get lost in it. You may know the route from your office to the photocopying room, and from your office to the loo. But if you suddenly needed to go straight from the photocopying room to the loo, then you could be in trouble!

Other problems in the office could include:

* Keeping things neat and tidy on your desk
* Keeping things filed in an orderly manner
* Dealing with complex tables of figures
* Reading diagrams
* Setting out your work neatly
* Analysing complex displays on a computer screen
* Seeing how to put theoretical knowledge to practical use

Space is closely allied with time, so as well as having difficulty in judging, say, the distance between yourself and a doorpost, you might also have a problem in estimating how long it might take you to get something done, or how much time you should leave to get to a meeting.

Problems with social interaction

If you find it difficult to negotiate 'social space', you might have difficulty in your interaction with colleagues or managers – a difficulty made worse if your relations with them are already tense because of your workplace inefficiency.

It could be that you find it tricky to 'strike the right note' when talking to people. You might come over as too distant or too familiar, you might seem to be treating serious matters flippantly, while at the same time failing to see a joke. You might find it hard to 'turn-take' in conversation, and you might make people feel uneasy by being noisy and loud, or by remaining unnaturally silent.

Other problems could be:

- Sitting or standing too close to people
- Not attending to what people say
- Talking off the point
- Yawning and looking bored
- Not picking up social signals, such as body language and facial expression
- Being dishevelled in appearance (buttons can be a problem!)

From all of the above, it is clear that dyspraxia causes a large number of problems – even without taking account of the fact that it is usually combined with some degree of dyslexic difficulty. However, as is the case with dyslexia, there are many strategies that can be adopted to reduce the effect of dyspraxic difficulties and make them more manageable.

DYSPRAXIA AT WORK: PROBLEMS AND SOLUTIONS

'I can have problems handling scientific instruments such as microscopes, and lab equipment generally. I've trained myself to work slowly and carefully and I've improvised two arm rests to help keep my hands steady.' *Jeannie, biologist*

'I seem to have no sense of direction. I can get lost even in an area I know well. I find it helps to pick out landmarks as I go along and fix them in my mind. Also before turning into a street, I look back the way I came and fix the image in my mind so I'll know which way to turn when I come back.' *David, travelling salesman*

'I have cupboards full of tools and bits and pieces of things I might need. But I can never find anything when I want it. I've solved this by going through all the cupboards and listing their contents on the computer. So now I can sit back and do a virtual search!' *Jon, handyman*

Complete the following checklist to see if your difficulties fit the dyspraxic profile. If you tick many of the boxes, you may like to seek further advice from one of the main dyspraxia organisations (see pages 186–187).

Everyday Dyspraxic Difficulties

Tick any items that apply to you.

Do you bump into things/people, and often trip over?	❑
Do you spill and drop things often?	❑
Do you find it difficult to do practical tasks such as:	
cooking	❑
DIY	❑
typing	❑
keying numbers on the telephone	❑
driving a car	❑
riding a bicycle	❑

Do you find sports difficult, especially team and
    bat-and-ball games? ❑

Do you find it difficult to judge distance and space? ❑

Are you over/under sensitive to:
                sound ❑
                smell ❑
                taste ❑

Are you generally disorganised and untidy? ❑

Do you have a problem with prioritising tasks? ❑

Do you find it hard to finish off work? ❑

Do you often lose things/fail to remember where
    you have put things? ❑

Do you have problems working against
    a background of noise? ❑

Is there a delay between hearing something
    and understanding it? ❑

Do you find it difficult to interpret body language? ❑

Do you interrupt people often? ❑

Assessing dyspraxia: some general considerations

If you think you might be dyspraxic and are considering
having an assessment, you first need to think carefully
about *why* you want the assessment. If you have severe
co-ordination problems and are applying for a Disability
Living Allowance to fund assistance with everyday tasks,
such as cooking, then you need to be assessed by an
occupational therapist.

But if your co-ordination problems are not severe, and
you are looking for general support and training to make
you more efficient either in study or in working life, then

you need to be assessed by a dyslexia assessor *who is also knowledgeable about dyspraxia.* (Always check that the assessor does have expertise in *both* dyslexia *and* dyspraxia; some assess for the former only.)

It may, of course, be appropriate to have both a dyslexia/dyspraxia and an occupational therapy assessment, but it is best to start with the one that seems to have greater relevance to your immediate needs. An occupational therapy assessment can be arranged through your GP; a dyslexia/dyspraxia assessment usually has to be arranged privately (see Chapter 4).

KEY TIPS

- If you have ticked many of the boxes in the Dyspraxia Checklist, consider having a formal assessment to see if you have significant dyspraxic difficulties.
- If your physical co-ordination problems are severe you may be eligible for the Disability Living Allowance. For you to qualify for this Allowance, your GP must refer you to an occupational therapist for an assessment.
- If your physical co-ordination problems are not severe but you need general support and training, you can arrange to be assessed privately by a dyslexia assessor who is also an expert in dyspraxia.

CHAPTER 4

ASSESSMENT

In recent years information on dyslexia and dyspraxia has become more widely available, and, as a result, adults of all ages are now coming forward in ever greater numbers to request assessments. Some people need an assessment because of difficulties with their work or study; others simply want a better understanding of themselves. It can take some courage to have an assessment, but it is very rare to hear of anyone who has regretted their decision to do so.

DYSLEXIA ASSESSMENT

There are two types of dyslexia assessment: *screening tests* and *full assessments*. A screening test may give some indicators that you are dyslexic, and encourage you to go on to have a full assessment. However, screening tests have limitations, the most serious one being that they do not always pick up the more subtle types of dyslexic difficulty. So if you come out as 'not dyslexic' on a screening test, *this does not necessarily mean that you are not dyslexic*; it may simply mean that you have compensated for your difficulties sufficiently well to fool a relatively simple test.

As regards a full assessment, there are four important things you need to know:

- How to find an appropriately qualified assessor
- How to fund the assessment
- What happens in the assessment
- What the assessment report should tell you

How to find a qualified assessor

A dyslexia assessor will belong to one of the following groups:

- Occupational psychologist
- Clinical psychologist
- Educational psychologist
- Research psychologist
- Specialist dyslexia tutor

It is by no means the case, however, that every member of these groups specialises in assessing adult dyslexia. Even less is it the case that they will have particular expertise in *workplace dyslexia* assessment and consultancy. Occupational psychologists are experienced in doing workplace needs assessments, but rarely have expertise in dyslexia. The other four groups will be able to offer a dyslexia assessment, but rarely have experience in workplace needs assessment and employer consultancy.

There are, however, a small number of practitioners, coming from each of the above five groups, who have chosen to specialise in workplace dyslexia. These practitioners will be able to offer a combined *diagnostic dyslexia* assessment and *workplace needs* assessment. At the time of writing, the largest cluster of such practitioners is in London, the remainder being scattered somewhat sparsely around the country.

If you are unable to locate an assessor who has the expertise to do a combined diagnostic and workplace needs assessment, then you will have to do each part of the assessment separately with a different assessor.

FINDING AN ASSESSOR

1. Begin by looking at the list of workplace specialists given in this book on pages 183–184.
2. Next, contact your local branch of the British Dyslexia Association (BDA) or Dyslexia Action (DA).
3. If you can't find a local practitioner, look further afield. Telephone the BDA or DA in London or any other large centre, and be prepared to travel.

If you already have a diagnostic dyslexia assessment, and you only require a workplace needs assessment, this can usually be arranged through your local Access to Work Business Centre.

CHOOSING AN ASSESSOR

Once you have found the name of a practitioner who appears to have the appropriate expertise, you will need to telephone that person and ask if he or she can offer you an assessment. This is a crucial moment. An assessment is expensive, it is probably something you will only do once in your life, and the results will affect the rest of your life. How can *you* judge if the assessor is right for you?

You will need to have prepared particular questions to ask the assessor in your initial telephone conversation. As a dyslexic person, who may be lacking in confidence and weak in communication skills, you may not find it easy to 'interrogate' a professional person about what they do. But think for a moment: when a barrister or a large commercial organisation employs the services of an expert practitioner in any field, they are not content with just a recommendation. They inquire about the experience and expertise of that practitioner. So why shouldn't you?

QUESTIONS TO ASK

Here are some suggested questions – try to ask at least half of them.

- What proportion of your practice is with adult dyslexics? (At least 50 per cent is desirable.)
- What proportion of your practice is given to workplace dyslexia consultancy? (At least 25 per cent is desirable.)
- Can you produce a detailed workplace needs report as well as a diagnostic report?
- Can you recommend a tutor who specialises in workplace dyslexia training?
- Can you advise my employer on the provisions of the Disability Discrimination Act 1995 in relation to dyslexia?
- Can you advise my employer on reasonable adjustments in the workplace?

Try to avoid asking these questions in either an aggressive or a timid way. All you are doing is making a reasonable request for information, so just put the questions straightforwardly, saying you have a few specific things you need to check out. If the practitioner objects to being questioned, put a black mark down against his or her name. If you make a mess of your enquiry on the telephone, then just e-mail the practitioner with your questions.

Funding the assessment

An assessment is expensive – several hundred pounds – and so you may need help with raising the funds. There are several possibilities:

Private health insurance

Some private health insurance companies will fund assessments by chartered psychologists. In the case of BUPA, your GP can refer you directly to a psychologist; other companies may require you to follow a more complicated route via a hospital consultant. In either case, *do not rely* on the NHS to find a psychologist for you. Locate an appropriately qualified psychologist yourself in the way suggested above, and give the name of this particular psychologist to your GP/consultant.

Employer

Employers are often willing to fund an assessment, either directly or through their own health insurance. They may, indeed, have a legal obligation to do so in certain circumstances.

Access to Work

You may be able to arrange a workplace needs assessment through your local Access to Work Business Centre. It is important to note that, even if Access to Work agrees to fund your assessment (and training), *you do not have to accept the assessor or trainer that this organisation offers you.* You can request an assessor and trainer of your own choice; you need only provide evidence that your chosen practitioner is suitably qualified.

Dyslexia organisations

Some of the main dyslexia organisations offer bursary schemes (see pages 184–185). Also try the local branch of the British Dyslexia Association.

Charities

Try educational or local charities, or church organisations. Or get yourself sponsored for an assessment.

Higher education institutions

If you are combining work with study at a college of higher education, you could qualify for a Disabled Students Allowance. The Allowance does not cover the cost of the initial assessment, but many colleges are prepared to pay for this themselves. If all else fails, it may be worth trying to borrow the money for the assessment, because, if you are awarded the Allowance, you will receive financial aid worth several thousand pounds for tuition and equipment. Discuss the position with the Dyslexia Support Tutor at your college.

What happens in an assessment?

You may be feeling a little nervous about going for an assessment, perhaps worrying that something dreadful about you will be revealed. But, as far as you can, contain your nervousness: the most likely outcome of an assessment is that difficulties which you have been struggling with for a long time will be recognised, categorised and explained, and that you and your employer will be given advice on how to manage them.

THE INTERVIEW
Before meeting you, the assessor will already have spoken to you and your employer on the telephone, and will have collected background information from both you and your line manager. He or she will begin the session by asking you in more detail about your difficulties and also about your areas of strength. Of particular interest will be your workplace difficulties, and the types of strategies you have in place for dealing with them. You will also be asked if you have any suggestions as to ways in which your employer could give you help and support.

THE TESTS
You will then have a busy couple of hours or so doing assessment tests. These are *not* the sort of tests that have a pass or fail mark; they simply measure your ability on different scales, just as a tape measure measures your height. If you feel you are becoming fatigued during this part of the session, request a few minutes' break.

The tests fall into two groups: *cognitive tests* and *literacy tests*.

Cognitive tests

These are divided into four groups:

- Verbal skills (e.g. reasoning ability and vocabulary)
- Visual perception (e.g. doing jigsaws)
- Working memory (e.g. recalling numbers)
- Information processing speed (e.g. copying symbols)

The profile of results on these tests will indicate (a) whether you have dyslexic difficulties and (b) into which category, or categories, of dyslexia these difficulties fall. The tests will also give indications of dyspraxic difficulty.

Literacy tests

These include:

- Reading words out loud
- Reading a passage of text out loud
- Reading a passage silently, for comprehension
- Spelling
- Writing for several minutes

Some of these tests may be timed, but this does not mean that you have to race through them. The assessor will want to get an idea of your *normal* rate of reading and writing. So, unless otherwise instructed, work at your usual pace.

One final test to mention is a test of phonological skills. As explained in Chapter 2 (page 16) phonological sequencing (the ability to sequence sounds) is an important feature of auditory dyslexia. To test this ability, the assessor will probably ask you to read some nonsense words. Unlike real words, these cannot be recognised by their shapes, so the only way for you to read them is to sequence their sounds. Here are a few for practice:

fep

klud

clost

spront

truglop

welgruny

depistabul

vintaspridolity

DYSPRAXIA AND VISUAL STRESS

As well as testing for dyslexic difficulties, the assessor will also be on the lookout for indications of dyspraxia and visual stress. This will not necessarily involve more tests, but you may be asked to fill in checklists, and to read a passage of text using overlays of various colours.

FEEDBACK

At the end of the session, the assessor will explain the assessment results and their implications, and outline an individual training programme that would be of benefit to you. He or she will subsequently contact your employer to discuss reasonable adjustments that could be put in place in order to help and support you at work.

TOP TIP

If, during the assessment, your anxiety level rises to such a degree that you can't concentrate properly on the tests, speak openly to the assessor about this. Your abilities cannot be reliably measured if you are 'frozen' with anxiety. It is best to pause for a few moments to let your nerves calm down. Don't be embarrassed about this or feel you need to apologise. Close your eyes for a few seconds and take one or two deep breaths.

What the assessment report should tell you

No two assessors write their report in the same way, but every report should contain certain basic information. Below is a typical report structure which, as you can see, clearly differentiates between (A) background information, (B) report of assessment results, (C) recommendations to the employer, and (D) appendices with additional information.

Report of Diagnostic and Workplace Needs Assessment

A. BACKGROUND:
- Reason for referral
- Background information
- Client's report of difficulties and coping strategies
- Concerns expressed by the employer

B. DIAGNOSTIC (COGNITIVE) ASSESSMENT:
- Test results in summary
- Test results in detail
- General conclusions

C. WORKPLACE NEEDS ASSESSMENT:
Recommendations for:

- Individual training programme for client
- IT support
- Referral, if appropriate, to other experts (dyspraxia, visual stress, counselling)
- Reasonable adjustments which the employer can make
- Sources of general advice and help

D. APPENDICES:
a) Notes on tests used
b) Information sheets on dyslexia, dyspraxia, visual stress

Part of the assessment report will use technical language. Tests will be described, and scores given in detail. The following information should help you understand this part of the report.

You will recall that there are four types of cognitive tests:

- Verbal skills (e.g. reasoning ability and vocabulary)
- Visual perception (e.g. doing jigsaws)
- Working memory (e.g. recalling numbers)
- Information processing speed (e.g. copying symbols)

It is the pattern of scores on these tests that indicate whether your difficulties can be categorised as *predominantly*:

- Auditory dyslexic
- Visual dyslexic
- Processing speed dyslexic
- Dyspraxic

Remember that most people have a mixture of difficulties. The grid below shows you the most typical patterns. The four types of test are shown along the top of the grid, and the four types of difficulty down the left-hand side. The symbols used in the grid are:

✓ = good test score

x = poor test score

(x) = possible poor test score

Category of Difficulty	Type of test			
	Verbal	Perceptual	Working Memory	Info Processing
Auditory dyslexia	✓	✓	x	x
Visual dyslexia	✓	x	(x)	x
Processing speed dyslexia	✓	✓	✓	x
Dyspraxia	✓	(x)	(x)	x

You may find that some scores in both the cognitive and literacy tests are given in *percentiles*. Percentile scores are on a range from 0–99. An average percentile score falls between 25–75.

0 _____ 25 _____ 75 _____ 99
   low   average   high

So, if your reading, for example, is at percentile 50, you are exactly average.

Your assessment report should do full justice to both your strengths and weaknesses. If you have any difficulty understanding your report, or if you feel that it in some way misrepresents you, don't hesitate to contact the assessor to discuss your concerns.

KEY TIPS

- For a full assessment of your needs you should try to locate an assessor who specialises in both *diagnostic dyslexia* assessment and *workplace needs* assessment.
- If necessary, the two parts of the assessment can be done by different assessors.
- To find a suitable assessor, look at the list of workplace specialists given at the back of this book, or contact your local British Dyslexia Association or Dyslexia Action branch, or your local Access to Work Business Centre.
- Prepare a list of questions before contacting the assessor to ensure that he/she is the right person for your specific needs.
- Funding to pay for the assessment may be available from your health insurance, employer, Access to Work, dyslexia organisations, charities or higher education institutions.

PART B

▓

IMPROVING SKILLS

All the strategies suggested in this section are ones that you can adopt and put into practice yourself. However, it is always useful to get some help from an expert if you can. The practitioner who carries out your dyslexia assessment should be able to recommend an experienced dyslexia trainer. It is possible that your employer or your local Access to Work centre will fund such training.

Alternatively, you could approach your employer with the suggestion that you be allocated a mentor from within or outside your organisation. The mentor would not necessarily need to be a dyslexia expert, but would need to be someone who could take on board the advice given in this book and help you put it into practice. Or perhaps there is someone in your family or within your circle of friends who could work through this section of the book with you.

If you have to rely on self-help, so be it. But you don't have to be isolated – contact your local branch of the British Dyslexia Association to get details of your local adult support group.

CHAPTER 5

ORGANISATION

Consider a typical working day. When you set out for work in the morning, do you feel calm and confident about the day ahead? Do you know roughly what your day's schedule will be, and have you prepared in advance any papers or files that you will need? When you reach the office, is your desk neat and tidy, or does it look more like an earthquake zone? Can you see at a glance what work is urgent for that day, or do you just pick up the first thing you see and start doing that? In other words are you, or are you not, well-organised?

Being organised is *the* fundamental workplace skill – an absolute must, whatever the nature of your job, whatever your talents, whatever your difficulties. If you can manage to get the overall *structure* of your day right, if you can set up *routines* that will ensure things get done on time, and if you can *plan and prepare* for particular tasks, then you will be able to keep control of your workload, alert people well in advance if you are overloaded, and avoid the stress and fatigue that result from operating in a nightmare of chaos and confusion.

In this chapter you will find advice on:

- Scheduling routine tasks
- Keeping track of your workload
- Planning your work schedule
- Planning particular tasks
- Remembering things
- Finding things
- Giving yourself some treats

ESTABLISHING ROUTINES

The essence of efficiency is to have dependable routines. A routine that you don't always manage to follow is a far better thing than no routine at all. Not only do routines increase the likelihood of work getting done in a timely way, but they also act to reduce stress by giving form and structure to the working day.

It is interesting that people who work in creative professions – and who have no boss hovering over them – often stick quite rigidly to daily routines. Writers, for example, often adopt monastic routines of life when they are working. This gives a reassuring structure to the working day.

People's working days are very different. Some may be by nature unpredictable, but most contain many routine elements. Think carefully about your own job and write down a list of tasks that you repeat every day, or perhaps every week. Consider whether you have established efficient routines for carrying out these tasks, or whether you tend to switch from one task to another in a random way.

The following case study illustrates how a chaotic working day can be brought under the discipline of a clear routine.

Case study: Order out of Chaos

Krishnan, an 18-year-old student with dyslexic difficulties, took a temporary holiday job as a clerical assistant in the office of a large commercial company. He was allocated a number of tasks, each of which was relatively simple. However, he found it difficult to organise his working day so that he got through these tasks in a timely and efficient way. He would start doing one task, get interrupted, then start doing something else – and forget about the first task. Or he would neglect an urgent task and instead do something that was relatively unimportant. He felt continually anxious that he had made a mistake or forgotten something vital. And if he was unexpectedly given some extra work, he would panic about how he was going to find the time to do it.

Fortunately, Krishnan had been assigned a supervisor who was knowledgeable about dyslexia. This supervisor was able to sit down with Krishnan and work out an efficient work routine for him.

Krishnan's work routine
The first stage in the process of organising Krishnan's

work routine was to make a list of all the tasks that Krishnan had to do *every* day. These were to:

- Open and distribute post
- Check telephone messages
- Receive e-mails and faxes from clients and distribute them
- Check expenses claim forms
- Send out information and advertising literature
- Keep all printers, fax machines and photocopiers supplied with paper

The supervisor recommended that Krishnan allocate particular times of day to particular tasks. She suggested that his first task in the morning should be to check that there was enough paper for the computers, photocopiers and fax machines; otherwise he would keep getting interrupted all day by people asking him to supply paper.

His next task would be to check the post and any faxes or emails that had come in overnight. But after that there was no need for him to keep interrupting his work every time a new fax came in, or a courier arrived with a parcel. He simply needed to decide on particular times during the day when he would 'make his rounds' with faxes and deliveries, and let his colleagues know exactly when these times would be.

With his supervisor's help, Krishnan drew up a detailed Daily Schedule. *The morning section* of it looked like this:

9.30   Check that faxes, computers, photocopiers are supplied with paper

9.45   Check incoming e-mails and telephone messages, and e-mail a note of these to colleagues as appropriate

10.00   Open post and sort letters for distribution
Collect any faxes received overnight and sort for distribution
Distribute post and faxes as appropriate

10.45   Check expenses claims forms

11.15   Second round of fax/parcel distribution

11.30   Coffee break and five minutes' relaxation

11.45   Any other current or urgent tasks

12.45   Third round of fax/parcel distribution

1.00   Lunch

Thus the first part of Krishnan's morning was now allocated to routine tasks that were vital to the smooth running of the whole office. After the coffee break he had a lengthy period of time to do other, less routine tasks, or perhaps urgent work. The coffee break itself was an essential part of his routine. If he was very busy, he might be tempted not to take a break – but this would be a mistake. Research shows that workers who take regular breaks finish jobs more quickly, and more efficiently, than workers who just go 'slogging on', however tired they are getting.

Some routine tasks – for example, filing, ordering stationery – needed to be done on a weekly rather than daily basis. So Krishnan kept a separate schedule for each day of the week. Then he could schedule the stationery order for, say, Monday, and the filing for Friday.

Keeping to this Daily Schedule meant that Krishnan was now able to focus on particular tasks that had to be done at particular times, and this kept him from wandering randomly from one task to another. It was not vital that he kept exactly to the times given – that would be too much to ask in a busy office – but it was important that he kept his basic routine intact.

TOP TIPS

Arrange to have a period of time each day
when you are not interrupted by colleagues
other than for urgent business.
Use this time for tasks that need particular
focus and concentration.
If you have to leave a task half-done, make a
quick note before leaving the task of how far
you have got with it, and jot down any ideas
you have in mind about what is still
to be done.

KEEPING TRACK OF YOUR WORKLOAD

It is not difficult to keep track of routine tasks once you have them efficiently scheduled. But the rest of your workload may be less easy to manage. Your desk may have disappeared under a pile of letters, e-mails, memos, reports, files and notes to yourself, all demanding your attention. Where do you start?

The first priority is . . . prioritising.

You need to clear space on your desk for three work trays and one filing tray. Preferably, the trays will be of different colours – say, red, blue, green and yellow.

- Label the red tray 'NOW'. This tray is for work that must be done immediately.
- Label the blue tray 'TODAY'. This is for work you aim to do during the day.
- Label the green tray 'PENDING'. This is for non-urgent work.
- Label the yellow tray 'FILING'. Clear this tray once a week.

All the papers on your desk should be put into one of the four trays, and then you need to follow a strict checking routine: check all three work trays at the beginning of the day, at lunchtime and at the end of the day. You will gradually have to move work forward from PENDING to TODAY to NOW. (If you work in a paperless office, then set up an equivalent system on your computer.)

Action list

It is not enough just to have all your papers in the right trays. When you come into work in the morning, you need to decide *exactly* in what order you are going to do things that day. So you need to draw up an Action List for the day. Your Action List is separate from your Daily Schedule. The Daily Schedule is your timetable for *routine* tasks; the Action List prioritises *non-routine* work.

You could write your Action List on an A4 sheet, preferably of coloured paper so that it stands out from the rest of the papers on your desk. Put the day and date at the top of the paper, and use different colours for different days.

Suppose, for example, that there are two items in your NOW tray. Write 'NOW' on your Action List and then write down the two tasks in the order in which you are going to do them.

If there are three items in your TODAY tray, write 'TODAY' on your Action List and then write down the three tasks in the order in which you are going to do them.

Check if you have any appointments to keep or meetings to attend during the day. If so, write down the times and venues on your Action List.

Has anything else occurred to you that you want to do that day? Perhaps you need to get some information from a colleague on a particular matter? If so, make a note on your Action List of when to do this.

Your Action List is your 'bible' for the day. Check it, as you do your trays, three times a day:

- At the beginning of the day
- At lunchtime
- At the end of the day

Clearly cross off each task when it is completed. If some urgent tasks are still outstanding at the end of the day, simply put the List in the NOW tray, so that these tasks will be attended to first thing the next day.

This system will help you to organise your work schedule efficiently. At the beginning of each day you will be able to see at a glance what work you have to do that day, and allocate time for it. Also, because you check through your PENDING file every day, you will not suddenly be taken by surprise one day by a large amount of work that needs doing. You will be able to plan ahead.

PLANNING YOUR SCHEDULE

When planning your future work schedule, you need to take into account two things:

- All the work waiting for you in your three work trays
- Future appointments/meetings/business trips

If you work on computer, you can keep your work schedule on the computer and set alarmed reminders for meetings and work deadlines. Give yourself a reminder for meetings at least two days in advance, and for work deadlines at least one week in advance.

If you don't have a computer, get a month-by-month work planner, and pin up the sheets for the coming three months on the wall in front of you, or in some other clearly visible spot. Enter, in blue, all future appointments, meetings and business trips. Enter, in red, all work deadlines.

Meeting deadlines

So far so good. But just knowing when things have got to be done is not enough. You have to make sure you actually meet the deadlines. Suppose you have been asked to write a report on complaints made by customers in a particular three-month period, and how these have been resolved. You have been given a fortnight to produce the report. You have to decide roughly how long it will take you to collect the material you need and to write the report. Let's say you calculate you will need five hours. You must ensure that you will have that five hours available during the coming two weeks.

If you look back at the Daily Schedule that Krishnan drew up (page 57), you will see that the latter part of his morning was not allocated to a particular task, but was left to be used flexibly, according to need. So, if Krishnan needed to schedule in five hours for producing a report, he could utilise this time slot, and work on his report for one hour each morning for a week. This would leave him plenty of time in hand before the fortnight deadline if he found that five hours was insufficient for the task.

TOP TIP

If you find you are getting tired and losing concentration while doing a particular task, such as checking invoices, switch for a while to another, less demanding, task, such as photocopying.

PLANNING PARTICULAR TASKS

Planning a work schedule is planning on a large scale. But planning is also necessary for smaller-scale tasks, such as report writing. Having scheduled time to write a report, how do you plan to actually carry out this task?

A good way to start is to carefully think through *precisely* what the task will involve. Many tasks can seem overwhelming if you look at them as a whole. But if you can break them down into stages, and then concentrate on tackling one stage at a time, they become more manageable.

Taking the customer complaints report as an example, you might identify the following stages:

1. Check out customer complaints log
2. Collect relevant files
3. Read through files and make notes
4. Discuss particular cases, as necessary, with colleagues or customers
5. Make preliminary notes for report
6. Plan structure of report
7. Write report
8. Check report

The report-writing task has now been broken down into eight distinct stages. As you work through the task, concentrate fully on the stage you have in hand at any one moment; don't dart back and forward between, say, reading through files and planning the report.

In summary, when tackling any large project, don't rush into it: think, plan and prepare.

TOP TIP

To keep yourself organised, invest in a pocket PC. This is a hand-sized organiser that can store your diary, set alarmed reminders for appointments, create action lists, record messages and store documents.
See pages 173–174 for more information.

REMEMBERING THINGS

During a typical working day, you will have to take in a lot of information. People may give you instructions or information, or request some action from you. You may take part in discussions or meetings where something comes up that you want to remember later. You might have a bright idea yourself about something and want to keep a note of it; or you might need a reminder of something you need to do that day.

It is no good just hoping that you will remember all these things. What you need is a small *personal notebook* that you can easily keep in your pocket or bag. Into this notebook put anything and everything that you need to be reminded of. Check your notebook at least three times a day.

A page of your notebook might look like this:

> *Phone client re work deadline
>
> *Arrange date for meeting with Human Resources
>
> Get a hand-held spell checker?
>
> *Phone IT adviser
>
> Find out about new business directory
>
> *Get files for line manager
>
> Training seminar – directions:
> Victoria line to Goodge Street, turn right outside tube, and first left into Store Street

The starred (*) items are urgent and need to be transferred to your Action List as soon as possible. As you deal with each item in your notebook, cross it out clearly.

FINDING THINGS

Many dyslexic people report that they are constantly losing things, or forgetting where they have put them. Keys, letters, notebooks all mysteriously go missing, and files are never where they should be. If you have this problem, you will know how much exasperation it can cause.

Filing

Let's start with files. To be easily found, files need to be (a) clearly labelled and (b) filed in the correct place.

Begin with the labelling.

Get some coloured labels and mark file names clearly on them. On ordinary files put the label on both the front and back of the file, placing it in the top right-hand or left-hand corner where it will easily be seen in the filing cabinet. On box files put a label on the spine as well.

To make your filing even more efficient, put a second label on the files showing the initial letter(s) of the file name only. For example, mark a file labelled 'Expenses':

<table>
<tr><td>EXPENSES</td><td></td><td>EXPENSES</td></tr>
<tr><td></td><td>or</td><td></td></tr>
<tr><td>E</td><td></td><td>EXP</td></tr>
</table>

You could also cue the position of E in the alphabetic sequence by showing letters before and after E:

c d **E** f g

The main reason why files are lost is that they have been mis-filed. Dyslexic people have difficulty in following sequences, and that includes the alphabet. To help you file things correctly, keep an alphabet arc on top of the filing cabinet.

You may also like to make yourself a pocket-sized alphabet arc to carry around with you. It will be helpful if you have to find a street in an A–Z, or look up a name in a telephone directory.

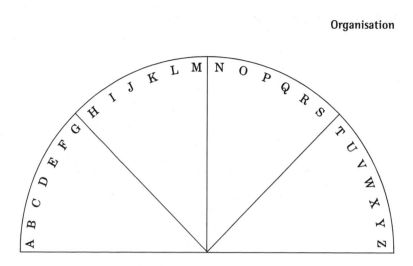

Keeping track of possessions

If you keep forgetting where you have put things – your keys, diary, glasses – assign a particular place on your desk or in your workplace where you will *always* put these things, and train yourself to put them there. You might like to get a small coloured tray or basket to hold them.

GIVING YOURSELF A TREAT

So far the emphasis in this chapter has been on scheduling work; now it's time to talk about putting moments of pleasure in your work routine.

It may be that you have already taken measures to make your office pleasant, perhaps by putting up pictures or installing plants. But there may be many other small things you can do to give yourself a moment of pleasure when doing a routine task.

The following suggestions come from clients and colleagues of mine:

'Get a pleasing paperweight. I used to use whatever came to hand – a stapler or anything. Then, in a museum, I saw some beautiful polished stones with lovely grain and colour. So now I use these as paperweights, and they are a constant delight.'

'I loathe filing, and the filing cabinet was a hate object. So I cut out beautiful pictures from magazines and pasted them onto the file dividers. So now I find filing quite a pleasure.'

'I seem to spend a lot of time in tedious meetings. Recently, instead of getting irritable about this, I've started using the time to do some deep breathing and muscle relaxation exercises. It helps me not just through the meeting, but through the rest of the day as well.'

'I keep a small octagon of coloured glass on top of my computer. The colours are beautiful and they change as the light changes, or when I shift my position. It brightens up even the dullest day.'

Another way to release yourself temporarily from the office routine is to spend a few minutes meditating, or just in silent reflection. Even if you work in a busy office, you can use headphones to give yourself some moments of silence and peace. Enjoy!

Most of the advice given in this chapter has been focused

on office routines. However, the general organisational principles described above can be applied to – or adapted to suit – almost any type of job. Whether you are managing a household, organising a conference or running a country, you need to have clear routines, well-thought-out work schedules, good time management, efficient memory aids, and an organised working area – as well as opportunities for rest and relaxation.

KEY TIPS

- Prepare a *Daily Work Schedule* to cover routine daily tasks.
- Use separate trays to prioritise tasks and label them 'Now' (*do at once*), 'Today' (*do sometime today*), 'Pending' (*non-urgent*), 'Filing' (*sort once a week*).
- Write an *Action List* to establish the order of each day's tasks – routine and non-routine.
- Check your *Daily Work Schedule,* trays and *Action List* three times a day.
- Prepare a *Future Work Schedule* to cover deadlines, meetings and appointments; keep it on your computer or pin up a month-by-month work planner.
- Use different colours to distinguish the separate tasks.
- Break down large tasks into stages and concentrate on one stage at a time.
- Use a notebook or pocket PC to help you remember instructions and information.
- File documents alphabetically and use an *Alphabet Arc* to help you locate them.
- Keep a special tray for personal items such as keys, diary, or glasses.
- Decorate your workspace with pictures, ornaments, etc. – these will give moments of pleasure and reduce stress.

CHAPTER 6

READING AND UNDERSTANDING

Most jobs involve some element of reading. This could range from reading a report to reading a signpost. Whatever the task, efficient reading usually comes down to three things:

- Reading words accurately
- Understanding and recalling what you read
- Reading numbers and mathematical data accurately

READING WORDS ACCURATELY

Different types of words cause different problems for dyslexic readers.

Short words cause a problem because they often look like other short words. Examples are:

where were wear

who how

hear here

Irregular words cause a problem because they can't be read phonetically (by their sounds), and are difficult to recognise quickly, if your visual memory is poor. Examples are:

thorough

cautious

nought

You could give your memory a hand by compiling your own *personal dictionary* in which you note down words that constantly give you trouble. If you keep your dictionary on the computer, you can easily list words alphabetically. (Check if your word processing programme has a 'sort' function that will do this for you.) Update the list regularly and print it out so that you can keep it handy.

Long words have the advantage that they are usually more regular in spelling, but they cause a problem simply by being long. As explained earlier (pages 16–17), when we read a long word, we use a component of our memory, the *mindless memory loop,* to store the sounds of the word in the correct sequence. But the loop has a limited capacity and can soon become overloaded and inefficient. It then starts missing out parts of words or jumbling sounds together in the wrong order. This is why you may find you have read *inhospitable* as *inhospable* or *hippopotamus* as *hippotopamus*.

To tackle this problem, you'll need to adopt one of the organising principles described in the previous chapter, namely: break down a large task into sections or stages. So when faced with a long word, such as interdenominational

don't make a vague stab at it. Break it down, either mentally or with a pencil, into its constituent parts or syllables:

in-ter-de-nom-in-a-tion-al

Then just say the syllables carefully one after another.

If you have difficulty knowing where one syllable ends and the next starts, try singing the word to a well-known tune, such as 'Auld Lang Syne'. Each note of the song represents a syllable:

Should	auld	ac-quaint-ance	be	for-got
in	ter	de nom	in	a tion al

If you spend a little time looking at some long words, for instance in a newspaper article, you will see that, if you break the words down into their syllables, the same syllables occur again and again at the beginning, and at the end, of the words.

Common syllables at the beginning of words (prefixes) include:

in, com, re, dis, de, pro, pre

Common syllables at the end of words (suffixes) are:

tion, sion, ibility, ness, ful

If you familiarise yourself with the common prefixes and suffixes shown in the list below, you will be able to read long words more quickly and accurately, as it will only be the middle of the word that is unfamiliar. You may like to put this list in your personal dictionary.

Another useful thing to put in your dictionary is a list of difficult words that crop up continually in the work documents you read. If you find yourself struggling again and again with 'necessitates', 'uneconomical' or 'referring', note these down and practise writing them, syllable by syllable, at odd moments when you're sitting on a bus or waiting for a train.

LIST OF COMMON PREFIXES AND SUFFIXES, AND THEIR MEANINGS

COMMON PREFIXES

Prefix	Meaning	Example
ad	to, towards	advance
con, com	together	companion
contra	against	contradict
de	down	descend
dis	not	disbelieve
ex	out	exterior
in, im	in, into	interior, implode
inter	among	international
mis	wrongly	mispronounce
mono	single	monopoly
per	through	pervade
poly	many	polysyllabic

post	after	post-war
pre	before	pre-war
re	again	review
sub	below	submarine
syn, sym	together, harmonious	synchronise, symphony
un	not	unhappy

COMMON SUFFIXES

Suffix	Meaning	Example
able, ible	capable of, fit for	eatable, edible
er, or	doer of an action	painter, director
ed	shows past time	called, shouted
ing	shows present time	I am reading
ess	shows feminine	lioness
ful	full of	fearful
ion, sion, tion	(1) state of	depression, confusion, elation
	(2) event	explosion, election
ist	practitioner	chemist
ity	quality of	tranquillity
less	without	fearless
logy	study of, science of	geology
ness	state of	happiness

UNDERSTANDING AND RECALLING WHAT YOU READ

The twin tasks of understanding and recalling written material represent something of a 'chicken-and-egg' situation: you can't understand a text unless you recall at least the gist of it as you are reading it; and you can't recall a text if you didn't understand it. Your working memory is on overtime in this situation. It has to somehow grasp the key points of what you are reading, and store them in the thoughtful memory box (see page 14). It's not the job of your memory actually to decide what the key points are – your reasoning power does that – but your memory is in charge of holding them safely, and accessibly, in your mind for future reference.

Can you at this moment recall what you read in the previous paragraph? If you are dyslexic, very possibly not. Dyslexic people have to put a good deal of effort into the basic mechanics of reading, that is reading words accurately. So the first time they read through a text, they are concentrating on simply recognising the words. This leaves them with insufficient memory capacity to *understand* and *recall* the text at the same time. So they have to re-read the text, perhaps several times, to gain a proper comprehension of it. This, of course, means that they are slow readers.

Reading workplace documents

It is possible to develop strategies to speed up reading, and to improve comprehension and recall.

(A) READING WRITTEN INSTRUCTIONS

When you begin a new job, it is likely that you will be given written instructions for the various tasks you have to do. Quite probably the instructions will have been written by someone who has no problems with reading, and so no thought will have been given to making them 'dyslexia-friendly'.

Take a look at the instructions in the box below. These were given to a young dyslexic woman beginning a new job as a clerk in a large translation agency.

Responding to telephone calls:
If a client calls to commission a translation, you need to fill in all the details on the commission form, and e-mail it on to the Translations Unit. Also put the details in the commission log.

If a client calls to check on work in progress, transfer him/her to the Translations Unit. If a client makes a complaint, take the details on the complaint form, and e-mail it on to the Translations Unit. Also put the details in the complaints log.

If a translator who is looking for work telephones, send him/her the general information leaflet and an application form.

If one of our regular translators telephones with a query about anything, transfer him/her to the Translations Unit.

If a potential client calls to request information about the organisation, take full contact details and send the general information leaflet. Also, e-mail the details to our Advertising Unit, and enter call in query log.

If you find yourself confronted in your job with complex 'wordy' instructions like these, you should approach your employer and request that instructions be presented in a clearer format. Dyslexic people are often able to understand information more readily if it is presented visually rather than in linear text – so a flow chart, like the one opposite, might be a good solution.

TOP TIP

Note roughly how long you can read before becoming tired and losing concentration. Half an hour?
Then organise your schedule to allow you to read in half-hour time slots.
After each half-hour, either take a short break or switch to a less demanding activity.

(B) READING REPORTS

Reading a lengthy report can be a daunting task. To make it manageable, you need to apply the principle recommended earlier for tackling any major piece of work: break it down into stages.

A well-written report will be divided into sections with clear headings, and, with luck, a summary of the report contents will be given at the beginning. If you look at the report structure presented on page 47, you will see that the report is divided into four main sections:

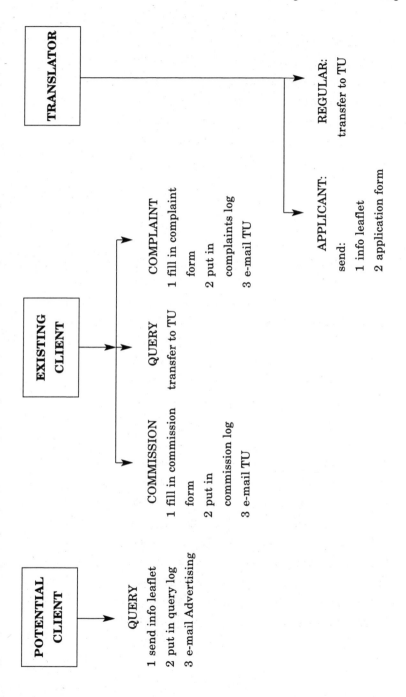

TRANSLATOR

EXISTING CLIENT

POTENTIAL CLIENT

REGULAR:
transfer to TU

APPLICANT:

send:

1 info leaflet

2 application form

COMPLAINT

1 fill in complaint form

2 put in complaints log

3 e-mail TU

QUERY
transfer to TU

COMMISSION

1 fill in commission form

2 put in commission log

3 e-mail TU

QUERY

1 send info leaflet

2 put in query log

3 e-mail Advertising

Background
Diagnostic (cognitive) assessment
Workplace needs assessment
Appendices

Within these four main groups, there are sub-sections, all clearly labelled. This highlights the vital importance of having some idea of the *structure* of a report before you delve into its *contents*.

Understanding structure

As an exercise in understanding structure, look back at Chapter 2 of this book (Dyslexia at Work) and write down a summary of its structure. To do this, first read the introductory section to get a general idea of what the chapter is about. Then note the structure in detail by skimming through the chapter and writing down the main headings.

The first main heading you will see is in capitals: AUDITORY DYSLEXIA, and throughout the chapter you will find further headings in capitals, such as VISUAL DYSLEXIA. So these are the main sections.

Now look in more detail at the first main section, AUDITORY DYSLEXIA. Within this section, you will find some sub-headings:

How does auditory memory work?
Auditory memory and phonology
Auditory memory at work

If you go through the whole chapter in this way, noting the headings and sub-headings, you will have the whole structure of the chapter clearly laid out before you:

AUDITORY DYSLEXIA
How does auditory memory work?
Auditory memory and phonology
Auditory memory at work

VISUAL DYSLEXIA
Visual perception
Visual memory
Visual dyslexia at work

PROCESSING SPEED DYSLEXIA

VISUAL STRESS

DO YOU HAVE A PROBLEM?

So, if you have to read a lengthy report, make a structural plan of it first, and *keep this plan beside you*, clearly visible, as you start to read the report for content. This will help you to put what you're reading into a meaningful structure – and this will aid both your understanding and recall.

TOP TIPS

You can make documents easier to read on a
computer screen by choosing the colour,
format, print size and line spacing that suits
you best.
Also, you can colour, italicise or embolden
keywords.

If you print out documents, use coloured paper
to avoid 'white paper glare'.

Understanding content

Having got a clear idea of the structure of a report, you
now need to focus on the content, that is, the detailed
information given in the report. To do this, take one
section of the report at a time, read it through carefully,
and highlight *keywords*.

Keywords exercise

As an exercise in understanding content, look at the
passage below, which is an extract from Chapter 2 (pages
12–14) of this book. Taking each paragraph in turn, focus
on identifying keywords that will indicate the main points
in the paragraph. You can then use the keywords to make
yourself a short summary of the passage. At the end of this
chapter you will find the passage again with the keywords
I have chosen, and the notes I have made.

(But please, try the exercise yourself before looking at these.)

There are two types of auditory memory: long-term memory and short-term memory:

- Long-term memory is used for remembering things on a more or less permanent basis – for example, the words of a poem we learnt as a child, and can still remember.
- Short-term memory is used for remembering things for a limited period, perhaps just for a few seconds – for example, remembering a telephone number, or some instructions we've been given. Here are a couple of short-term memory tasks for you to try:

Task 1. Read through the following list of words ONCE only, and then try to remember them without glancing back at the list:

lion, apple, table, snow, knife, light, coat, paper, hammer

Task 2. Read through the following sum ONCE only, and try to work out the answer in your head.

Add 8 and 4, divide by 2, and multiply by 5

If you are dyslexic, you may have a particular difficulty with these tasks, because, in auditory dyslexia, it is this short-term memory that is inefficient. And it can be inefficient in two ways. To understand this, we need to look in more detail at the workings of the memory system.

Look back at tasks 1 and 2 above, and you'll see that they were slightly different. In task 1, you just had to recall some information. In task 2 you had to both recall information (the sum given to you) and at the same time work on the information, that is, work out the answer to the sum in your head.

In task 1, your memory was passive: it functioned simply as a storage memory. In task 2, your memory was active; it operated as a working memory.

In dyslexia, both the storage and working components of the memory system can be inefficient. The diagram below will help you to visualise how these components work together and what can go wrong.

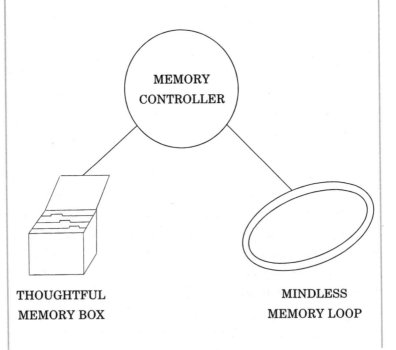

THOUGHTFUL
MEMORY BOX

MINDLESS
MEMORY LOOP

The memory controller at the centre of the system is the active working component of memory: it inspects any information coming into the memory system and works on it appropriately. It is helped in its work by two 'assistants': the mindless memory loop and the thoughtful memory box, both of which are storage systems.

The loop is like a fan belt – it has no brains and simply rotates at the command of the controller, mindlessly repeating information it is given. The box, however, is intelligent – it can store information it receives from the controller in a logical 'easy to find' way.

Recalling what you've read

One of the best ways of recalling what you read is to *think* about what you read (question it, criticise it, relate it to your own experience). The more thought you give to a particular topic, the stronger the memory trace of that topic in the brain. And the good news is that, if you have gone through the processes described above – noting the structure of a text, identifying keywords, making notes – you will already have done a lot of useful thinking. Rather than just reading mechanically, you will have carefully analysed the text from the point of view of both structure and content. You will have followed the logical sequence of ideas in the text and made decisions about which ideas you find most important. All this will be of immense help to your memory.

However, there are some additional strategies you can use to fix the content of what you read in your memory. Suppose you were trying to remember the information given in the passage quoted above on how memory works. You could try these strategies:

Association

To remember the components of auditory memory – controller, mindless memory loop and thoughtful memory box – associate each of them with a different room in your house or flat. Imagine the controller as a high-powered business type working away at a desk in the living room. Imagine the mindless memory loop as a gormless individual lying in bed all day listening to the same tapes over and over again. Imagine the thoughtful memory box as a university type studying all day in his or her room. Think of them as a family and wonder how they might get on together. Your memory will do much better at remembering this family scenario than just a plain list of auditory memory components.

Visualisation

Imagine yourself journeying inside the brain and visiting the auditory memory section. The controller greets you and invites you to shadow it throughout its working day. It turns out that this working day is quite a frantic affair. The controller is constantly receiving messages from other parts of the brain, all demanding to be remembered.

Some of these messages appear initially to be of little interest to the controller: it hurls them into a rotating loop without a second glance. Here they revolve around a few times, and then either the controller retrieves them, or the loop hurls them into a waste paper bin. Occasionally, the loop breaks down and the controller then has to scoop out all its contents and set it in motion again.

Other messages seem to be of more interest to the controller: it studies them for a few moments before labelling them and filing them carefully in a large box.

Towards the end of the afternoon the controller suggests that you take over from it for a short time, while it takes a tea break. Good luck!

Dramatisation

Imagine that you are going to give a lecture on the workings of auditory memory. You aren't going to write out the whole lecture, but speak from notes. Your keywords will serve as notes. Just rehearse your lecture once or twice in your mind, and then speak it into a tape recorder. Listen to your recording and think how you could have done it better.

TOP TIP

Text-to-speech software can read e-mails, web pages, and documents to you out loud. For more information see page 174.

READING NUMBERS AND MATHEMATICAL DATA ACCURATELY

Numerical data are often presented in complex tables or graphs. To deal with data of this sort, you need to be able to read numbers accurately, and to have strategies for reading complex visual displays of information.

Reading long numbers accurately

With a pencil, break numbers up into small chunks of two or three figures. So 758423741924 becomes:

75 84 23 74 19 24

or

758 423 741 924

Or look for bits of the number that are easy to remember:

198457435 = <u>1984</u> 57 435

2388771355 = 23 <u>88</u> <u>77</u> 13 <u>55</u>

674789512 = 674 <u>789</u> 512

Read each segment of the number twice. Do this carefully and then move on. Try not to keep on checking the number again and again. This will only snarl up your mindless memory loop.

Reading tables of figures

Numerical data are often presented in tables, such as the following:

No. of translations per month broken down by language											
Lang	Month											
	Jan	Feb	Mar	Apr	May	June	July	Aug	Sep	Oct	Nov	Dec
French	12	14	08	16	22	13	19	12	21	22	17	11
Spanish	10	18	11	15	03	10	22	14	29	21	14	16
German	19	24	18	28	31	22	15	14	28	35	17	20
Dutch	28	31	25	18	22	29	15	19	17	26	25	18
Italian	16	18	12	15	26	23	20	18	28	20	21	50
Greek	04	02	08	10	16	15	07	00	00	06	11	10
Russian	28	33	29	22	18	23	30	21	28	25	19	12
Polish	06	11	13	10	09	12	06	11	05	12	09	02
Danish	04	10	08	09	01	03	11	14	09	13	10	06

It is easy to lose your place in a mass of figures like this, and to make mistakes. To avoid this, you need to put some structure on the table, to divide it up in some way, so that you know where you are in it.

Here are some ways of dividing up the table (see page 90):

- Concentrate on the horizontal lines under each row of figures. Under every third row, draw an extra-thick line. Three-row segments are easy to work with, as you always have a 'beginning, middle and end'. Each three-row segment represents three languages.
- Colour each three-row language segment a different colour.
- Use two rulers, or two straight-edged pieces of paper placed at right angles to each other, to help you find a particular point in the table – for example, the number of Greek translations in April (10) or Russian translations in November (19).

No. of translations per month broken down by language												
Lang	Month											
	Jan	*Feb*	*Mar*	*Apr*	*May*	*June*	*July*	*Aug*	*Sep*	*Oct*	*Nov*	*Dec*
French	12	14	08	16	22	13	19	12	21	22	17	11
Spanish	10	18	11	15	03	10	22	14	29	21	14	16
German	19	24	18	28	31	22	15	14	28	35	17	20
Dutch	28	31	25	18	22	29	15	19	17	26	25	18
Italian	16	18	12	15	26	23	20	18	28	20	21	50
Greek	04	02	08	10	16	15	07	00	00	06	11	10
Russian	28	33	29	22	18	23	30	21	28	25	19	12
Polish	06	11	13	10	09	12	06	11	05	12	09	02
Danish	04	10	08	09	01	03	11	14	09	13	10	06

TOP TIP

If you are reading a table of figures on the
computer, you can italicise or embolden
sections, or vary the font size,
as well as using colour.

Analysing statistical data

If you have to read statistical material presented in
visual form, such as tables, graphs, bar charts or pie
charts, begin by getting an overview of the material.
Carefully read the headings of the graph, table, and so on,
to be clear in your mind *exactly* what information you are
being given. Then look carefully at the labels on the
graph axes, the column headings, etc. These are often in

small print and may contain easily confused measurements, such as 'cm' and 'mm' (centimetres and millimetres).

Also, consider whether *all* the information given in the visual display is of interest to you, or whether you can focus on one particular section of it. For example, using the table shown above (page 89), if you just want to compare the number of translations done in March with the number done in September, then you could colour in the two relevant columns. Similarly, if the same information was shown in the form of a graph, you could colour in the two relevant lines on the graph. This would make it easy for you to refer again to this information at a later date.

Keywords exercise (from pages 83–85)
My own keywords and notes:

There are *two types of auditory memory*: *long-term memory* and *short-term memory*.

Long-term memory is used for *remembering* things on a more or less *permanent* basis – for example, the words of a poem we learnt as a child, and can still remember.

Short-term memory is used for *remembering* things for a *limited period*, perhaps just for a *few seconds* – for example, remembering a telephone number, or some instructions we've been given. Here are two short-term memory tasks for you to try:

Task 1. Read through the following list of words ONCE only, and then try to remember them without glancing back at the list:

lion, apple, table, snow, knife, light, coat, paper, hammer

Task 2.   Read through the following sum ONCE only, and try to work out the answer in your head.

Add 8 plus 4, divide by 2, and multiply by 5

If you are dyslexic, you may have a particular difficulty with these tasks, because, in *auditory dyslexia*, it is this *short-term* memory that is inefficient. And it can be *inefficient* in *two ways*. To understand this, we need to look in more detail at the *workings of the memory system*.

Look back at tasks 1 and 2 above, and you'll see that they were slightly different.

In *task 1*, you just had to *recall* some information. In *task 2* you had to both *recall* information (the sum given to you) and at the same time *work on* the information, that is, work out the answer to the sum in your head.

In *task 1*, your memory was *passive*: it functioned simply as a *storage* memory; in *task 2*, your memory was *active*; it operated as a *working* memory.

In *dyslexia, both* the *storage* and *working* components of the memory system can be *inefficient*. The diagram below will help you to visualise how these components work together and what can go wrong.

The *memory controller* at the centre of the system is the *active working component* of memory: it inspects any information coming into the memory system and works on it appropriately. It is helped in its work by *two* 'assistants': the *mindless memory loop* and the *thoughtful memory box*, both of which are *storage systems*. The *loop*

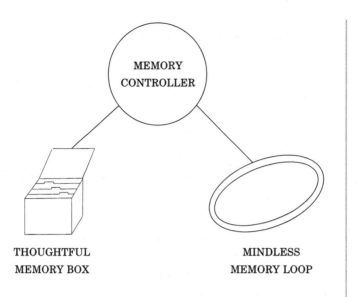

THOUGHTFUL   MINDLESS
MEMORY BOX   MEMORY LOOP

is like a fan belt; it has no brains and simply rotates at
the command of the controller, *mindlessly repeating*
information it is given. The *box*, however, is *intelligent*,
and can *store information* it receives from the controller
in a *logical* 'easy to find' way.

Notes on the above:

AUDITORY MEMORY
Distinguish between:

> long-term memory (LTM) for permanent recall
> short-term memory (STM) for temporary recall

Auditory dyslexia = poor STM

STM does two things:

> (1) actively works on information
> (2) passively stores information in two ways:

(a) mindless memory loop for a few seconds

(b) thoughtful memory box for a longer period

Any or all of the above can be inefficient.

KEY TIPS

- Break long words into syllables, if necessary singing the word to yourself to distinguish the syllables.
- Use a notebook to make a *Personal Dictionary* and write down problem spellings – especially ones that crop up often.
- Memorise *prefixes* and *suffixes* and their meanings.
- Carry your *Personal Dictionary* with you and memorise spellings when you have a free moment.
- Ask to have detailed instructions/information presented visually, for example as a flow chart.
- To understand a long report, write down the headings and sub-headings to give you its *Structural Plan* and highlight *key words* within each paragraph.
- Use Association, Visualisation and Dramatisation to help you recall what you have read.
- Break a long number into small chunks and highlight easy-to-remember ones.
- Divide complicated tables of figures into easy-to-manage three-row sections and use different colours to distinguish them.

CHAPTER 7

SPEAKING AND LISTENING

It may not be obvious at first sight that dyslexia might interfere with your ability to speak and listen. And certainly it does not interfere with your actual physical ability to do these things. But it might hamper your ability to express yourself clearly, and to follow what other people are saying.

You may find, for example, that you often forget names, or can't find the right words to express your meaning. Perhaps you have a tendency to 'ramble' when you are speaking, and easily lose the thread of your thoughts when you are trying to relate or explain something to other people. You may constantly go off at tangents and get lost in detail.

Similar problems can arise with listening. You may have difficulty following the gist of a conversation or discussion, and find that you have instantly forgotten some instructions that have been given to you. You may keep interrupting people, feeling that, if you let them go on talking too long, you will forget what they have said — and what you yourself want to say in reply.

One of the main features of dyslexia is poor short-term memory, in particular poor auditory (or hearing) memory. When we are speaking, or listening, to someone, our auditory short-term memory is constantly in play. Some dyslexic people who have very good verbal abilities compensate well for their memory problem when they are speaking, and so come over as good communicators; but few dyslexic people avoid difficulties with listening.

If you have problems with reading and writing, at least you have the luxury of retiring to a corner somewhere and struggling with these tasks in private; but if you have problems with speaking and listening, there is nowhere to hide. You are out there on public display, facing other people, trying to follow what they are saying to you and, at the same time, formulating your reply. However, there are some things you can do to make all this easier.

IMPROVING SPEAKING SKILLS

In a work context, improving speaking skills depends on, firstly, *good preparation* for any situation in which you will be required to speak, and, secondly, an *assertive attitude*.

Good preparation

In social situations you can't predict what topics of conversation might come up, but in the workplace you will often know in advance that you will be expected to express an opinion on a particular occasion about a particular topic. You can prepare for this in advance by making a few notes to yourself, perhaps in your personal notebook, to remind you of the points you will want to make.

Preparing to give instructions

Suppose you have been asked to give a new member of staff instructions about his or her job. This is something you can easily prepare for in advance. Make notes, either in a bullet point format or in a flow chart, of the information you will need to impart. Then go through your notes with the new employee, giving more detail or answering queries as required.

Preparing for meetings

Many people – even the most articulate – feel nervous about speaking in meetings. If this normal nervousness is compounded by dyslexic difficulties, and the lack of confidence that often goes with them, then you have a recipe for 'meetings avoidance syndrome'.

To make meetings more agreeable, there are a number of things you can do, not just before the meeting, but also during and after it.

Before the meeting, do careful preparation. Read any documents that will be discussed at the meeting, and make your own brief notes on them. Also make a note of any comments that you will want to make. If possible, discuss particular points informally in advance with colleagues who will be at the meeting.

During the meeting, you may feel nervous, but just allow yourself to be nervous. Put your anxiety on the 'back burner' as far as possible, and try to focus on the content of what is being said. Keep your eye on your notes and try to make your points at the appropriate moments.

It often helps if you have rehearsed some useful phrases. For example, if you haven't managed to intervene in a discussion, seize the moment when the discussion seems to be coming to an end, and say: 'I have a couple of points I would like to add before we leave this topic.'

If someone asks you a question, and you can't immediately get your thoughts together to answer it, play for time. Say: 'Well, that's a very interesting question that requires some thought.' Then pause for thought. If you still can't think of an answer, say: 'Can I get back to you on that – I'd like to consider it further.'

If you find yourself rambling on in the meeting, and people are making impatient movements, just say: 'Sorry, but this matter is rather complex – perhaps it's better if I e-mail you my thoughts on it later.' This will allow you to cease talking with good grace.

Of course, I don't advise you to use the *same* phrases at every meeting, but rather to have in your arsenal a repertoire of phrases that can get you through an awkward moment.

After the meeting, if you feel that you didn't manage to say what you wanted, or that you said it in a muddled way, don't spend the rest of the day feeling frustrated and annoyed with yourself. Just put the points you wanted to make in an e-mail, and send it to your colleagues with a note saying you've thought over what was said at the meeting, and you have some comments that you feel it is important to make. At the end of the day, what matters is that you find a way to make your views known. You will earn respect for this.

Preparing to give a talk

It may happen occasionally that you are asked to give a talk or make a presentation at a meeting. You may feel confident about doing this – or you may feel a sense of total panic. If the latter, you can be sure that you are not alone. Public speaking is something that does not seem to come naturally to most human beings. It gets easier with practice, but that is not much comfort when you make your first attempt at it.

There are two important things to remember: firstly, thoroughly prepare your material, and secondly, however ghastly you feel during the talk, just keep on talking. Your audience will only really be interested in *what* you say; *how* you say it will soon be forgotten. They may notice that you are nervous, but this will not loom as large in their minds as it does in yours. To be a good speaker you don't have to be a confident speaker – but you do have to be on good terms with your nervousness.

Once you have prepared your material for your talk, practise giving the talk to yourself, using a mirror and a tape recorder, or video recorder. This will enable you to:

- Get the timing of the talk right
- Hear if any part of what you say sounds muddled or repetitive
- Check your posture and gestures
- Check if you are making some eye contact with your audience (in this case yourself)

Preparing for job interviews

One situation in which you only have *one* chance to say what you want to say is a job interview. For that reason, it is all the more important to prepare carefully for such an interview.

You may not know exactly what questions you will be asked, but you can probably make a guess at the sort of subjects that will be of interest to the interview panel. They will probably include:

- Your previous job history
- Why you want this particular job
- What talents you can bring to it
- Your ambitions for the future

You can download typical interview questions from the Internet.

A day or so before the interview, jot down a few notes to yourself on the points you want to make, and rehearse the interview in your mind. If possible, role play the interview with a friend or family member. Practise walking confidently – but not jauntily – into a room and sitting composedly in a chair. Then practise walking out of a room in a dignified way. A job could be won or lost on the basis of your posture and manner.

In the interview itself, make eye contact with the interviewers when you are introduced to them. If you don't understand one of their questions, try not to get flustered, but calmly ask them to repeat it. Don't feel you have to rush your replies; you will earn respect if you seem to be putting some thought into your answers. If they do ask you a question to which you have already prepared an answer, don't recite the answer as if you are reading from a book, but try to speak naturally. If one of the interviewers seems unfriendly or aggressive, interpret this as being his or her problem – and rise above it.

At the end of the interview, you may be asked if you have questions or concerns you want to raise. Try to think of one of two, because if you just say 'no', that might seem as if you are not taking much interest in the job. You could, for example, ask what opportunities the job would afford for further training. As far as possible, you need to engage with the interviewers in a mutually informative dialogue.

Assertiveness

In Chapter 3, it was suggested that interaction between people could be described in terms of sharing a social space. Using this metaphor, assertiveness could be defined as taking up the space that is due to you – not letting yourself be crowded out of it by other people, and not taking up more than your fair share either.

Helpful here are the views of the Greek philosopher, Aristotle, who put forward the idea of the 'Golden Mean'. (The word 'mean' here has the sense of 'midpoint'.) Aristotle said that every virtue is a midpoint between two extremes. For example, courage is the midpoint between rashness and cowardice; proper pride is the midpoint between vanity and humility. Aristotle didn't mention assertiveness, but, had he done so, he might well have said that assertiveness is the midpoint between aggressiveness and timidity.

Using our spatial metaphor: if you take up too much space in a social encounter, you will appear aggressive and overbearing; if you take up too little space, you will send out a message that you are the sort of person who can be pushed around. But if you confidently occupy your *rightful* space, then you will be seen as assertive and authoritative.

Assertiveness in job interviews

The job interview is the first interaction between you and your potential employer. I've already suggested ways in which to prepare for the interview, and offered tips on general interview behaviour. But what about your dyslexic difficulties – are you going to mention these? And if so, can you talk about them in a confident and assertive way?

Some people prefer not to tell a potential employer that they are dyslexic. This may be because they think that this will 'put off' the employer, or because they don't think their difficulties are severe enough to matter, or because they haven't in fact realised they are dyslexic.

There is no easy answer to the question of whether or not it is to your advantage to inform a potential employer about your dyslexia. If you keep quiet about your difficulties this may help you get the job, but once in post, you will have to struggle alone with the difficulties without the benefit of help and support.

If you tell the employer about your dyslexia, there is a risk that this could lose you the job. However, if you get the job, then your employer would be legally obliged to make reasonable adjustments to accommodate your difficulties in the workplace. (More on this in Section C.)

Adjustments could include funding an assessment and providing training.

Let's assume that, on your application form, you have mentioned the fact that you are dyslexic. When you go for the job interview, this will almost certainly be something that the interviewers will want to ask you about. You will, of course, have had the chance to think in advance how to answer questions on this subject. In general, if you respond confidently, explaining the strategies you have in place to deal with your difficulties, then your dyslexia is unlikely to weigh heavily against you; but if you seem anxious or 'furtive' about your difficulties, then this could lose you the job. Try to talk more about your strengths and coping strategies than about your difficulties.

Employers have an obligation to make adjustments for dyslexic difficulties during the process of job application and interview. So, for example, you could ask to be given the interview questions in writing in advance of the interview, so that you can study them and formulate your answers. Also, if the interviewers know that you are dyslexic, they will be more understanding if you get yourself into a tangle while answering their questions. The fact that you find an interview difficult doesn't mean that you can't do a particular job – a clerical job, for example, doesn't depend on interview skills.

Assertiveness at meetings

It is not just in the job interview, but in the job itself that it is useful to alert people to your difficulties. Contributing to meetings can be difficult for a dyslexic person, but this is likely to be much less difficult if you have explained to your colleagues that you sometimes need a bit of extra time to formulate your thoughts. There will always be someone who thinks it's clever to make fun of your difficulties, but you may be surprised how helpful and supportive most colleagues are when they properly understand your problems.

At all times your best policy is to be assertive. Acknowledge your difficulties but show that you are pro-active in dealing with them. Your employer and your colleagues will respect you for this.

IMPROVING LISTENING SKILLS

Listening is in many ways similar to reading: you have to follow the general structure of what someone is saying to you, and pick out the key points. As we saw in Chapter 6, if your working memory is weak, this is not an easy task. In the workplace you are likely to have difficulty with understanding spoken instructions, following the gist of conversations and discussions, and taking notes in meetings.

One of the best ways to become a more efficient listener in the workplace is to take an assertive attitude to the problem. You can do this in a number of ways:

- Ask for instructions/information to be repeated or written down
- Ask people to speak more slowly
- Ask your employer to provide you with a digital voice recorder

TOP TIP

If you have to take orders or deal with complex
enquiries over the telephone, ask for e-mail
confirmation of the order or enquiry,
or send e-mail confirmation yourself.

Voice recorder

A digital voice recorder is a particularly useful aid to both
listening and memory. Compact and discreet, it can record
continuously for several hours. You can use it throughout
the working day to record meetings, talks, discussions
with colleagues, and instructions given to you orally. (You
will probably soon find that your non-dyslexic colleagues
will want one too!)

However, don't hand over all the responsibility for
listening to your recorder. You need to have it there as
backup in case you miss something important, but you
don't want to spend hours and hours listening to it. So, if
you are at a meeting, for example, always make your own
notes on the key points in the discussion and think about
what is being said – don't just sit back planning your next
holiday while the machine records everything for you.
Then, when you look back at your notes later, you will be
able to pinpoint where these are inadequate, and home in
on the relevant section of your recording.

TOP TIP

If your boss gives you a list of tasks to do,
or a set of instructions,
ask him or her to put these on tape or e-mail
them to you.

Note-taking

This is a particularly complex activity. It requires you to do a number of different things at the same time: listen, remember, follow the general structure of a talk or discussion, identify key points, and write notes.

If you attend a talk at which you will want to take notes, check beforehand if any handouts are available that show the general structure of the talk. Then, during the talk, you can focus on identifying key points in the content. Similarly, at a meeting, you may have been given an agenda or other relevant documents which provide you with the general structure of the discussion. If there is no paperwork to help you, listen carefully to how the speaker or chairperson introduces the talk or meeting. With luck he or she will begin with a summary of what is to follow. Note down the main topics, and keep an ear open for the speaker introducing each one of them.

Suppose that the theme of a talk is 'Making the workplace dyslexia-friendly'. Some of the topics discussed could be.

- IT support
- Allowing extra time for tasks to be completed
- Presenting instructions in flow charts

As the speaker progresses through the talk, you need to listen out for cues to the introduction of different topics. For example, after a few general introductory remarks, the speaker might say:

'First of all I'll discuss the advantages of IT support ...'

So in your notes, write in capitals:

1. IT SUPPORT

As the speaker goes through the different types of IT support, such as dictation software or mind-mapping programs, list these, with a separate letter for each. For example:

a. Dictation software
b. Mind-mapping programs

Coming on to the second topic, the speaker might say:

'Another way to help dyslexic employees is to allow them extra time to do things, for example ...'

So now write down your second main point in capitals:

2. EXTRA TIME

Then give the examples, each with its own letter, as before.

Concentrate on getting down the *main points*; you can listen to your recording of the talk later to fill in the details.

Avoid using unnecessary little words such as *and* or *but* in your notes. In the example given immediately above, you only needed two words – 'extra time' – to represent the 17 words spoken by the lecturer.

You can also use simple signs to represent long phrases. For example:

→	this leads to
✓	an advantage of this is
X	a disadvantage of this is
↑	there was an improvement in
↓	there was a deterioration in

Also, it's good to build up a set of abbreviations for common words. For example:

approx	approximately
dev	develop/development
effi	efficiency
admin	administrative/administration
acc	according to
rep	representative
stak	stakeholder

Start with a dozen or so abbreviations for words that you often use, and when you can reliably recognise these, add more to your list. You could keep the list at the back of your personal notebook.

With good note-taking strategies, a digital recorder as backup, and an assertive attitude, you should be able to cope well with most listening tasks in the workplace.

KEY TIPS

- Use a flow chart as an aid when giving instructions to other people.
- Prepare for meetings by reading background documents and note down any points/comments you want to make.
- Learn useful phrases to use if you get tongue-tied, such as 'Can I get back to you on that?'
- E-mail colleagues with any comments you didn't manage to make at a meeting.
- Prepare for talks by rehearsing in front of a mirror and/or using a tape/video recorder.
- Prepare for interviews by writing down/ rehearsing answers to likely questions.
- Practise walking and talking in a confident manner.
- Be assertive – not aggressive or timid.
- Ask for instructions to be repeated slowly, or – better still – written down.
- Use a digital voice recorder to record meetings, talks and discussions – and keep notes too.
- Note down the key words in any talk or discussion, and learn symbols or abbreviations for common words and phrases to save time.

CHAPTER 8

WRITING

Like reading, writing finds its way into almost every job imaginable. Office workers have to write letters and e-mails, an electrician has to fill in timesheets, a security guard needs to keep an incident log, and an artist has to correspond with galleries and clients.

In this chapter advice will be given on:

- Writing work documents
- Writing style
- Spelling and punctuation
- Filling in forms
- Writing numbers accurately

WRITING WORK DOCUMENTS

Work documents range from relatively short e-mails or letters to lengthy reports, portfolios or business plans. Whatever the nature of the document, you need to approach the writing of it in a systematic way. Firstly, you need to do all necessary *preparation and research* of your material; secondly, you need to *plan the structure* of what you are going to write.

Preparation and research

Make sure you are quite clear in your mind about *why* you are writing a particular document, and *what sort of material* needs to be included in it. If you are not clear about this, seek advice from your line manager or another colleague; otherwise you will waste time collecting irrelevant information.

Next, collect together the background material you need and keep it all together in its own filing tray. It may be that this background material consists of a daunting pile of papers and files. In such a case, employ the principle of doing things stage by stage:

- Take one item at a time
- Study it carefully
- Mark keywords
- Make a *brief* note of the information you feel is relevant to your purpose

TOP TIP

If you have to read through, say, six
documents, each 10 pages long and separately
numbered, take a red pen and number all the
pages continuously from
page 1 to page 60.
Then you can quickly and reliably refer to a
particular page.

Planning structure

In this section we'll look at how to plan and structure
three types of workplace document: reports, letters and
memos. *Even if your work does not involve report-writing,
it is vital to read the advice given on this topic*. The
principles used in structuring a report are exactly the
same as those used in structuring a letter or a memo.

Reports

Report-writing can be a daunting task. One positive thing
that can be said about it, however, is that it is not as bad
as essay writing. In a report at least, you often have the
advantage of being able to structure your material under
clear headings, and to present information in bullet
points rather than in continuous text.

To illustrate the principles of report writing, let us
suppose that you have been asked to write a report
entitled:

'Dyslexic Difficulties in the Workplace'

Your research for this will probably have included reading some relevant articles and websites, and perhaps talking to dyslexic people who experience difficulties at work. So you will have a number of ideas on the subject in your mind. You will need to include in the report some – though probably not all – of the information you've gathered.

This is the moment for 'brainstorming'. Take an A4 sheet of paper and, without too much reflection, jot down ideas for the content of the report *just as they come to you*. When you run out of ideas, you might like to leave the results of your brainstorming on one side for an hour or two, or even overnight – additional ideas may come to you later.

Having written down all your ideas, consider how you can arrange them in *logical groups*. For example, suppose your brainstorming has produced the following list of workplace difficulties:

> slow reading
> forgetting instructions
> spelling
> missing deadlines
> forgetting appointments
> losing files
> writing logically
> understanding what you read

You could divide these difficulties into four main groups as follows:

Reading:	slow reading
	poor comprehension
Memory:	forgetting appointments
	forgetting instructions
Writing:	spelling
	writing logically
Organisation:	losing files
	missing deadlines

You can simply colour-code the groups on your original A4 sheet, but it is probably better to write the new list on a fresh sheet of paper, or on the computer.

Now that you have collected and grouped your ideas, your next task is to decide in which *order* to present them. It seems logical to put the two literacy groups together, so your final list would be as follows:

Reading:	slow reading
	poor comprehension
Writing:	spelling
	writing logically
Memory:	forgetting appointments
	forgetting instructions
Organisation:	losing files
	missing deadlines

You now have the structure for the main body of your report. So far so good – but more is needed. You need to write an *introductory* section explaining the purpose of the report, and you may like to add a section with *recommendations* for the employer. Finally you will need to sum up the contents of the report briefly in a *conclusion*.

The complete structure of your report will now be as follows:

TITLE:
Dyslexic Difficulties in the Workplace

INTRODUCTION:
Why you were asked to prepare this report
How you collected material for it

AREAS OF DIFFICULTY:
1. Reading
    a) reading slowly
    b) reading with understanding
2. Writing
    a) spelling
    b) writing logically
3. Memory
    a) forgetting appointments
    b) forgetting instructions
4. Organisation
    a) losing files
    b) missing deadlines

RECOMMENDATIONS

CONCLUSIONS

You now have before you a clear structure for the report that you are going to write, so you are ready to begin writing. All you have to do is to work your way methodically through your structure plan, elaborating on each topic in turn. The clarity of the report structure will not only help you to write the report; it will also help readers of the report to grasp its content quickly. The headings and sub-headings clearly signpost the logical progression of ideas, and you may also include 'signpost phrases' in the text such as:

Firstly, I would like to note...
Secondly...
Finally...

I would now like to turn to...
Another area of difficulty is...
Before I leave this topic...

As a result...
Consequently...
By contrast...

The general guidelines given above for report-writing will apply to most types of report. The two vital things to remember are: get the structure clear in your mind first, and then do the writing stage by stage.

TOP TIP

You can buy software programs that help with structuring written text.
See page 176 for more details.

Letters

A letter is usually shorter than a report, but its structure may be equally complex. *This means you need to do the planning for both in the same way.* When it comes to the writing, however, you have to summarise your ideas in a letter, rather than elaborate on them, as you would in a report. So if you wrote a letter to a colleague about your report on workplace difficulties, it could read as follows:

> Dear Colleague,
> re: dyslexic difficulties in the workplace
>
> I am writing to let you know about the report I have just completed on dyslexic difficulties in the workplace.
>
> I was asked to carry out this report by the Head of Training, and collected my material through interviews, web research and reading journal articles.
>
> I identified four main areas of difficulty: reading quickly with good comprehension, writing accurately and logically, memory, and organisational skills.
>
> I also made recommendations for ways in which the employer could give support in all four of these areas.
>
> Please let me know if you would like me to e-mail you a copy of the full report.
>
> Yours sincerely,

As you will see, this letter is very short, and yet it contains all the main points that were in the full report. This highlights the importance of always being clear about structure: you can't summarise information successfully unless you are completely clear in your own mind about how it 'hangs together'. So always prepare and plan your letters as if they were reports.

Memos

Just as a letter can be seen as a short report, a memo can be seen as a short letter. It has the same structure as a letter, but the information is given even more briefly, perhaps even in note form. Here is the above letter condensed into a memo:

> From: To:
> Date: 24th August, 2006
> re: Contents of report on dyslexic difficulties in the workplace
> Report commissioned by Head of Training. Based on interviews, web research and relevant reading.
> Four areas of difficulty identified: reading quickly with good comprehension, writing accurately and logically, memory, and organisational skills.
> Recommendations made for employer support.

WRITING STYLE

Writing is done for many different purposes, and it is important that the writing style chosen is suitable for the purpose in mind. To attune your ear to style, read through the following short texts. Read them aloud if possible.

1. EXTRACT FROM GINA'S DESCRIPTION OF HER DYSPRAXIC DIFFICULTIES (PAGES 29-30):

I've always been a very clumsy person. I'm forever bumping into things and tripping over or twisting my ankle. I've usually got a bruise somewhere and can't remember how I got it. I often put my clothes on inside out and have difficulty with buttons and zips. I'm very messy generally, embarrassingly so when I'm eating. And I can make a real mess of filling a flowerpot.

At school I wasn't very good at sports. I never learnt to dance either, or to ride a bike. I had about ten driving lessons, but then had to give up. I had enough problems working out what to do with my feet, let alone keeping an eye on what was going on outside the car.

2. EXTRACT FROM EXPLANATION OF DYSLEXIA (PAGE 3):

Some researchers adopt a 'narrow' definition of dyslexia: they view it simply as a difficulty with word reading (dyslexia means literally 'difficulty with words'), and they search for the cause of this. Other researchers adopt a wider definition. They view dyslexia as a syndrome, or group, of difficulties that includes problems with literacy skills, memory, perception, sequencing and organisational skills. Researchers who take this view tend to be less concerned with the cause of dyslexia and more interested in its effects.

3. EXTRACT FROM A REPORT BY A COLLEAGUE ON PROFESSIONAL DEVELOPMENT:

The consensus of opinion amongst dyslexia specialists is that henceforth it should be a requirement for all tutors to make application annually for a practising certificate, and that the certificate should only be awarded if tutors could demonstrate that they had engaged during the year in a significant number of professional development activities in a variety of contexts. It would be expected, for example, that tutors would engage in original research, contribute to journals and conferences, and maintain a high-level awareness of new developments in their professional field.

The three texts are markedly different in style. In Gina's description of her difficulties, she uses a very informal conversational style. In the extract from Chapter 1 of this book, I use a semi-formal style – not as loose as a conversational style, but not as dense as an academic or formal style. An example of a formal style is the report on professional development.

What distinguishes the three styles is the level of vocabulary used, the length of the sentences, and the complexity of the sentence structure.

In writing work documents, it is important to choose a style that is appropriate, and stick to it. Don't keep switching between a formal and conversational style as in the following example:

> 'I am writing to inform you that management has now issued a directive requiring all operatives *to make a bit more of an effort.*'

In general, try to avoid using long words where short ones will do.

SPELLING AND PUNCTUATION

As a preliminary, please look back at pages 72–75 in Chapter 6, and remind yourself of the advice given there about keeping a *personal dictionary* and *dividing up long words* into their component syllables. Also note the information given on common prefixes and suffixes. All these things will help your spelling as well as your reading.

Spelling

In your dictionary, keep a note of common words that

constantly trip you up. This might be because:

- They have irregular spellings: height
- They look like other short words: where were
- They sound like other short words: here hear

You can use little tricks to cue the spellings of these words:

- A h**eight** of **eight** inches
- They were w**here**? **here**!
- H**ear** with your **ear**

Also, keep a note of words that crop up frequently in workplace documents that you write. Some well-known demon words are:

referring	(double '**r**')
accommodate	(double '**c**' and double '**m**')
business	(**u**–s–**i**)
current	(**e**–n–t)
commitment	(double '**m**' and single '**t**'
facilitate	(i–**l**–i))
extrapolate	(**a**–p–**o**–l–**a**)
commission	(double '**m**' and double '**s**')
contemporary	(o–**r**–a–**r**)

Of course, if you are working on a computer, you can use the spell-check for these. If your e-mail system does not have a spell-check, write the message in a word processing document first, run the spell-check, and then cut and paste the text into your e-mail.

Finally, a reminder that, if you keep your personal dictionary on the computer, you can instruct the computer to sort your word lists into alphabetical order.

Punctuation

Punctuation can be a puzzle. If you feel its complexities are beyond you, at least observe some basic rules:

- Use commas to separate two parts of a sentence: When the sun shines, I feel happy.
- Start new sentences with a **C**apital letter and end them with a full stop.
- Use commas to separate items in a list: paper, pens, pencils, staples.
- Use a colon (:) to show you are about to give a list (see example above).
- Distinguish between: **its** = belonging to it (the car lost *its* wheel)

  it's = abbreviated form of 'it is' (*it's* a pity)
- Note how to indicate possession:

  For <u>one</u> person or thing: 's   one *horse's* tail

  Words to watch: names ending in –s (James's, Thomas's)

  For <u>two</u> persons or things: s'   (two, or more, *horses'* tails)

  Words to watch: irregular plurals men's, women's, children's

FILLING IN FORMS

Filling in forms is something that many dyslexic people dread. There is no way to make this tedious task pleasant, but you could do a few things to alleviate the misery.

First, assign a particular period of time – say half an hour – in which you will sit down with your form and a cup of coffee (or, if necessary, a stiff gin).

Secondly, skim through the whole form to get a general idea of the questions asked, and to see if there is any information you need to have by you as you fill in the form, for example, your National Insurance number.

Then, tackle the form page by page. Beginning with the first page, tackle that page section by section. In each section tackle one question at a time. Concentrate on exactly what is being asked.

Some questions will be straightforward requests for your contact details. Others may ask for numerical data, such as details of bank accounts. When writing such details, use the strategies suggested in the box overleaf for writing numbers accurately. Study very carefully – and calmly – instructions on the form telling you to miss out sections, or move on to later sections.

If some questions require a lengthy written answer, plan your answer and practise writing it first on a separate piece of paper. If you make a complete mess of part of the form, write out the relevant question(s) and your answer(s) on a separate sheet of paper and attach it to the form. State clearly on the form that you have done this. If, after half an hour, you haven't finished filling in the form, take a break and assign another half-hour to the task later. When you have finished filling in the form, check it through carefully.

WRITING NUMBERS ACCURATELY

If your job involves a lot of numerical work, for example entering numbers in tables, you will know that it is easy to make a careless error, especially if you are tired or distracted.

As noted earlier (pages 88–90) you can improve your accuracy in reading tables of data by creating three-row segments, and by using colour, italics or bold print to contrast one segment with another. These same strategies will also help when you are entering data into tables. Try to enter the data in manageable chunks, such as one row at a time, and check through each chunk of data once only.

TOP TIPS

When writing long numbers, write them down
in three-number chunks, and check each
chunk once before writing the next one.
Say the numbers out loud to yourself
as you write.
When you have written the whole number,
check it through once.

If you find yourself getting flustered with the
numbers, pause for a few seconds.
Remind yourself that you will get the number
right if you calmly and carefully follow the
above strategy.

Be aware that some numbers lend themselves to error. A good example is a number that has a lot of noughts in it. It's easy to confuse 20,000 with 200,000. (Use coloured markers to highlight each of the noughts in a different colour.) Also, if you are writing down long reference numbers that contain both numbers and letters, make sure you clearly distinguish 5 from S, and 1 from I.

This chapter, like all the previous chapters in Section B, contains many suggestions for improving your workplace skills. It might seem at this point that it is all too much to take in, and that the amount of advice you're being given is becoming more of a problem than your original difficulties! However, if you adopt the oft-recommended stage-by-stage approach, and aim to build good strategies into your work routine *gradually*, you will see a steady improvement in your efficiency.

KEY TIPS

- Prepare written reports by breaking the subject down into sections, based on the notes you made in your background reading.
- Choose an appropriate writing style and keep to it.
- Add problem words to your *Personal Dictionary* – irregular spellings (height/eight), easily confused words (where/were, there/their, here/hear), and 'demon' words (business, accommodation).
- Check instructions carefully before filling in forms.
- Deal with form-filling line by line – take regular breaks to avoid fatigue.
- Write long numbers in three-number chunks, checking each chunk carefully.
- Write numerical data a line at a time, checking before writing the next line.

CHAPTER 9

EMOTIONS

So far throughout this book the emphasis has been on the practical difficulties associated with dyslexia. Now it is time to turn to a different, but equally important, aspect of dyslexic difficulties: the painful emotions that they so often · engender – emotions such as *anger*, *confusion*, *frustration*, *anxiety* and *despondency*. Over the years, these emotions become entwined with the practical difficulties, producing a vicious circle of anxiety and inefficiency.

Fortunately, this circle can be broken. Many dyslexic people find that, once their difficulties have been fully recognised, they are able to start the process of building up skills and strategies to help them deal with their problems. As their efficiency and confidence increase, so their anxiety lessens, and their mood becomes more optimistic. This allows them to shift their attention away from their difficulties, and more towards their strengths, be these academic, social, practical or artistic.

MANAGING YOUR EMOTIONS

A vicious circle of difficulties and negative emotions cannot be broken overnight; change will come gradually. But you don't just have to watch and wait: there are positive things that you can do to improve your emotional state. You can learn strategies for managing frustration, reducing anxiety, increasing confidence, and remaining calm under stress.

Bewilderment and confusion

If you were fortunate enough to have your dyslexic difficulties recognised and explained when you were young, you were probably spared the pain of growing up – and perhaps growing old – feeling that your life was a hostage to a set of baffling inefficiencies. You would 'know your enemy' and be able to negotiate with it from a position of strength. You might even be able to make a friend of it.

If, however, you have spent years, indeed decades, struggling with a bewildering set of difficulties that trip you up at every turn, then you are likely to feel total confusion about yourself. In the words of James, the office worker whom you met in the first chapter:

> I think the worst part was not understanding what was going on. In some situations I'd operate quite well – in the office I'd be quite good at coming up with ideas for new ways of doing things, but when it came to actually doing them, I'd make a lot of mistakes. So one minute I'd

feel quite clever, the next a complete idiot.

It was like being two people – from moment to moment I wouldn't know which one would take over. It made me feel insecure all the time – I was a mystery to myself.

James's line manager echoed this confusion:

Well, frankly, I just didn't know what to make of him. He was totally erratic, not only in his work, but in his general attitude. It was hard to understand why he didn't make more effort. Presumably he didn't want to lose his job, yet half the time he acted as if he didn't care what happened to him. It was strange because he came over quite well at his job interview – bright and imaginative and well-motivated – but once in the job he seemed to go downhill quite quickly.

The confusion about James's difficulties was finally dispelled when he decided to have a dyslexia assessment. One of the main benefits of an assessment is that it not only gives a clear picture of the difficulties, but shows how they all relate to each other, and, in particular, to the underlying basic weaknesses, such as poor memory. In other words, it makes sense of them. Many people approach an assessment fearing that they will be pronounced 'a hopeless case' – and so they are very relieved to find that they actually have a well-recognised syndrome of difficulties, for which they can get specialist help.

If you, like James, have been struggling for years with a bewildering set of difficulties, you are obviously starting to try to understand and deal with them by reading this book. Getting a clear understanding of the problem is the vital first step on the road to managing it. See pages 192–194 for suggestions for further reading.

Embarrassment and shame

For a dyslexic person, life can be a series of embarrassments: forgetting names, writing crucial information down inaccurately, stumbling over words at meetings, taking twice as long as everyone else to do things. Over time, all these minor embarrassments can contribute to a growing feeling of shame, and eventually a dyslexic person can feel almost as if they have a 'guilty secret' – a secret that they must keep closely guarded, if they don't want to lose their job. And it can happen that the people closest to them end up guarding the guilty secret too. James's wife, Laura, found herself doing exactly that:

> I can't remember exactly the point when I first felt James was behaving rather strangely – I think it was more a gradual feeling that built up that he was keeping something from me. He seemed sort of shifty, as if he was ashamed of something. As time went on, I began to imagine all sorts of things – he was having an affair, he'd defrauded the company, he was just pretending to have a job. Well, you do hear about such things! In the end – I know it sounds ridiculous – I started to feel ashamed as well. If we went out together to some social do, I'd feel a dread that our secret would be found out.

Once the dyslexic difficulties are out in the open, they can be dealt with in an assertive way, rather than be hidden away like a guilty secret. In Chapter 7, assertiveness was defined as taking up your rightful amount of space in the world. In relation to dyslexia, assertiveness could be seen as allowing your dyslexic difficulties to openly occupy the space they deserve, and not be kept huddled and uncomfortable in some secret cupboard. Once 'out of the closet', they will not only seem less threatening to you, but other people also will be able to take proper account of them.

Frustration and anger

Frustration is one of the commonest emotions reported by dyslexic people. It's frustrating to have thoughts in your head and not be able to put them down clearly on paper. It's frustrating to have a strong opinion on a matter and be unable to express it eloquently at a meeting. It's frustrating to check your work again and again, and then find that it is still inaccurate.

Wherever you find frustration, anger is not far away. Anger that your efforts are not rewarded. Anger at your own inefficiency. Anger because other people don't understand or don't seem to care.

Obviously, once you begin to develop good strategies to manage your difficulties, your efficiency will improve, and so your frustration will lessen. And the energy that went into being angry can be diverted into more creative channels. In the short term, however, it is good to have some techniques in place to get you through the bad moments when you feel you could scream with frustration or lash out in anger.

Gina, the dyspraxic gardener whose difficulties were described in Chapter 3, describes how she managed to control her angry feelings:

> I used to get furiously angry about all my difficulties. I'm not by nature a violent person, so I never took it out on anyone else – it just stayed inside me, a sort of enemy within. I happened to read about a bank somewhere in America where the managers had a special room where they could go and break things when they were feeling frustrated or angry. So I thought, well fine, I haven't got a room, but I have got a garden, and scores of little plant pots. So, when I feel unbearably angry, I go and hurl a few of them against the wall. I find it's really helpful – it takes the edge off my anger.
>
> Also, I try and keep calm in situations where someone is getting impatient with me because I'm fumbling with change, or whatever. Instead of snapping at them I just calmly tell them I'm dyspraxic and have difficulty with some things. Probably half the time they don't know what dyspraxic means, but usually they pretend to, and stop acting impatient.

It's always a good idea to look for ways in which you can channel the energy of your negative emotions either into a harmless, if violent, activity, or into an action that alerts other people to your difficulties.

Despondency and depression

Despondency afflicts us all at one time or another, and it is not surprising that dyslexic people often feel despondent about their difficulties. Over time, despondency can deepen into depression, and this in turn makes it harder to tackle the difficulties in a positive way. However, where there is a way down, there is a way up, though initially one may need a guide to find it.

For a dyslexic person, the way up starts with gaining a clear understanding of the difficulties, either by reading, or by having an assessment, or perhaps simply by talking to a colleague who is knowledgeable about dyslexia. The next step is to begin a systematic programme to improve skills, either by reading a book like this or by working with a tutor or mentor. And, crucially, the painful emotions associated with dyslexia need to be brought out into the open, either through talking with friends or attending a dyslexia support group.

This is a long-term process, but one that has an 'upward', optimistic feel about it. Should you feel too severely depressed even to look for 'the way up', then you should consult your doctor to discuss possible treatment options, such as counselling, medication, or cognitive behavioural therapy.

Lack of confidence

There are two sorts of confidence: (1) confidence that you can do a particular task, and (2) confidence that, if you can't do a task, you will be able to state this openly and seek relevant help.

There are many work situations in which lack of confidence holds a dyslexic person back. Attending an interview or work review, speaking in a meeting, making a presentation – these situations make most people nervous, but for the dyslexic person there is the added worry that their difficulties will inhibit or prevent them from expressing themselves clearly. They also find it difficult to discuss their difficulties with other people, particularly managers, in an assertive way.

Training courses can present a particular problem. Here, the dyslexic employee is often required to take in a great deal of information in a short period of time, and the information may be presented in a way that is not dyslexia-friendly. It takes some courage to explain one's difficulties and ask for extra help on a training course where the rest of the participants might be complete strangers, and the trainer may know nothing about dyslexia. Thus, many dyslexic people avoid applying for training, with the result that they are held back in their career.

Suggestions for improving confidence have been given earlier in the book (pages 101–104).

Anxiety and stress

Anxiety and stress stalk the workplace like malicious gremlins. They take a particular delight in tormenting dyslexic people, whom they see as easy victims. These gremlins need to be tamed and taught kinder ways, and this can be done by a combination of long-term strategies and short-term tactics.

LONG-TERM RELAXATION STRATEGIES

As far as possible, organise your life in a way that allows you to 'build in' regular periods of relaxing activity. This could be: meditating, listening to music, walking, going to the gym, having a massage, going for a jog, doing a relaxation exercise. In other words, anything that gives your mind a break from thinking.

The mind is actually a very determined thinker: it thoroughly enjoys mulling over its store of memories, and equally delights in fantasising about the future and making plans for scores of possible eventualities. At the same time it applies itself vigorously to problem-solving, and throws up myriad ideas for solving your current cash-flow problem or doing something about the terrible state of the world. Most of all, perhaps, it enjoys worrying.

How can you call a halt to this incessant thinking and bring the mind into quietude and repose? The following two approaches work for many people.

Break the chain

Don't try to *force* the mind to be still. That will be very stressful! Just let thoughts come into your mind in the usual way. But, as each thought comes to you, note it just as you would a meaningless sound, and then let it go. The reason that the mind gets so busy is that every thought leads on, by association, to another thought, and so the mind is constantly racing along this chain of associations. By catching the thoughts as they come in, and putting them to one side without interesting yourself in them, you are breaking this chain, or at least making it much slacker. So the rhythm of your thinking will slow down, and your mind will begin to learn a habit of rest.

Focus the mind

Try to concentrate your mind wholly on what you're doing at a particular moment. If you're doing the washing-up, for example, and at the same time worrying about some problem at work, bring your concentration to the task in hand. This can act as a kind of meditation technique. Look at the saucer you are holding – have you ever really *looked* at a saucer? Note its colour and shape, feel its texture, and be aware of your own movements as you wash it and place it on the drying rack. Watch its colour brighten as a shaft of sunlight catches it. Enjoy a task well done.

The curious thing is that, having put your current workplace problem on hold while you delight in a saucer, you may find that a solution to the workplace problem suddenly comes to you out of the blue. How often do people say that they go to sleep wondering how to deal with some particular problem or situation, and, lo and behold, they wake up with the answer? The fact is that, even though the conscious mind may be at rest, problem-solving and idea-development continue very vigorously at an unconscious level. Many creative writers report that they don't actively plan books, they just wait for them to 'emerge'. Too much conscious thinking can actually interfere with creativity and problem-solving.

The above long-term strategies for stress reduction are aimed at bringing about changes in your general lifestyle.

They can, however, be applied in particular ways to your working life. As noted in Chapter 5 (pages 67–68), it is important to schedule periods of rest in your working day, and to have about you objects on which you can meditate with pleasure. You also need to keep control of your workload and tackle particular tasks in a stage-by-stage manner. These efficient working practices will in themselves act to reduce anxiety and stress, as you will be in control of events rather than floundering in a sea of uncertainty.

SHORT-TERM 'ANTI-PANIC' TACTICS

There may be particular moments when you're overcome by sudden anxiety or panic. At such moments it can feel as if the world is about to end. Your heart thumps, you begin to sweat, and a darkness descends upon you. There is no easy way to have a panic attack, but you could cling on to the knowledge that (a) it won't actually do you any physical harm, and (b) it won't last long. Your body has gone temporarily into 'fight or flight' mode in the face of some perceived threat, but if that threat is simply facing an audience, not a lion, your body will gradually calm down.

If you are in a one-to-one situation, or in a small group, when panic overtakes you, you could summon up your assertiveness and simply inform the people around you that you are suffering an anxiety attack, and ask for a glass of water. You may then find yourself able to continue more confidently. If you frequently experience debilitating panic attacks, ask your doctor to refer you to a clinical psychologist.

RELAXATION EXERCISE

Allow about 20 minutes for this exercise. Sit or lie in a comfortable position. Close your eyes and gradually become conscious of your body. Feel where it presses against the chair or the floor. After a few moments tense up the muscles in your feet, hold them taut for a few seconds, and then let them relax. Then tense up the muscles of your lower legs, and hold them taut before relaxing them again. Gradually move up through your whole body in this way, concentrating fully on each part of your body as you reach it: your upper legs, buttocks, abdomen, chest, back, shoulders, arms, hands, and finally your neck and facial muscles. Then tense up your whole body, remain taut for a few seconds and completely relax.

After a few seconds, imagine you are lying in a sunny meadow by the side of a gently flowing river. You feel the warmth of the sun on your body, you hear the pleasant murmuring of the river, you feel the caress of a gentle breeze on your face, and you smell the sweet scent of flowers. All around you wooded hills rise up, and above them the deep blue of the sky is flecked with white clouds. Thoughts come into your mind, but you don't hold on to them. You take each thought as it comes and cast it gently into the river to be borne away. You let your mind be filled simply with the rhythm of your breathing.

When the time comes to leave this tranquil place, make unhurried preparations. Turn your mind gradually to the real situation you're going to return to, tense and relax your muscles a few times, open your eyes and make contact with your actual surroundings. Sit quietly for a few moments and then bring your relaxation period to end.

Relief, determination and hope

If you are able to gain a proper understanding of your difficulties, and to get appropriate help and support for them, the negative emotions associated with undiagnosed dyslexic difficulties can be transformed into much more positive feelings: *relief* at having made sense of your difficulties, *determination* to work hard to improve your skills, and *hope* for a more rewarding future. Also, once the focus is taken off what you can't do, and transferred to what you can and might do, then there is more room for your natural talents and abilities to shine through. They can, in a manner of speaking, be more assertive, because they are not continually overwhelmed by your difficulties.

As you begin to work on improving your skills and managing your emotions, it is good to keep in mind that change comes not only gradually but unevenly. So expect to have good days and bad days – days on which you feel you have coped well with a situation, and days on which you feel you haven't coped at all. Try to avoid reacting too strongly to either success or failure. Neither elation nor despair will be helpful to you. Just take note of when things have gone well and when they've gone badly, and in each case calmly try to analyse why. It may help you to write your observations in a diary or notebook. And if you do feel a bit down, you can call to mind Winston Churchill's robust advice to himself in the darkest days of the Second World War: 'Just keep buggering on!'

If you feel you would benefit from talking through your emotions with a professional counsellor, you will find relevant advice on page 190.

KEY TIPS

- Avoid embarrassment by being open about your difficulties – then others can make allowances and lend support.
- Release anger and frustration by channelling it into harmless physical – even violent – activity.
- Counter despondency by taking practical steps to manage your difficulties; seek medical help if you suffer serious depression.
- Manage stress by practising meditation and relaxation techniques.

▓

HELP FROM THE EMPLOYER

This section of the book contains information that will be helpful if you wish to bring your difficulties to the notice of your employer.

The first chapter in this section tells you what sort of things you could expect your employer to do in order to give you help and support in the workplace.

The second chapter is a handy guide to dyslexia written especially for employers, so that they can inform themselves about the nature of dyslexic and dyspraxic difficulties, and the sort of adjustments they could reasonably be expected to make. *You could photocopy this chapter and give it to your employer.*

The third chapter explains your rights under the Disability Discrimination Act 1995, and gives examples of employment tribunal cases.

CHAPTER 10

HOW YOUR EMPLOYER CAN HELP

If you are dyslexic – or think you might be – then you could consider approaching your employer to discuss ways in which the latter may be able to help or support you in the workplace. Employers have a legal obligation to make reasonable adjustments for dyslexic employees; these adjustments could include arranging an assessment, funding relevant training and making changes to your job specifications and working conditions.

> All the information given in this chapter
> will apply to dyspraxic
> as well as dyslexic employees.

You may feel unsure about whether it would be in your interests to make your difficulties known to your employer. Only you can make a decision on this according to your circumstances, but it is important to keep in mind that, if you don't disclose your difficulties, you may be missing out on a package of help and support that could benefit you not only in your working life but in your everyday life as well. Also, getting appropriate training may make the difference between keeping and losing your job. Look back to Chapter 7 (pages 102–103) for advice on how to make an effective approach to your employer.

ASSESSMENT

An employer cannot know how best to help you unless your difficulties, and the effects they have in the workplace, are thoroughly assessed. The assessment process has already been explained in detail in Chapter 4, and your employer can find a list of organisations that offer assessment on pages 183–185. Remember that it is important to find an assessor who specialises in *workplace dyslexia* consultancy, rather than general occupational psychology.

TRAINING

Your assessment report should include recommendations for a training programme specifically tailored to your needs and the requirements of your job. The assessor may recommend a particular trainer, but, if not, your employer can find a list of training organisations on pages 183–185.

The training programme should include some or all of the following:

Oral and comprehension skills

- Presenting thoughts clearly
- Following verbal instructions
- Discerning key points in discussions
- Contributing to meetings
- Dealing with interviews and work reviews

Memory and concentration

- Improving memory for spoken and written material
- Remembering appointments
- Exercises to focus and sustain attention and concentration

Sequencing and organisational skills

- Dealing with alphabetical material
- Efficient methods of filing, storing and linking information
- Efficient work methods
- Planning work schedules

Reading

- Reading quickly with comprehension and recall
- Discerning key points in a text
- Following written instructions

Writing

- Clear, correct and coherent writing
- Spelling rules, grammar and punctuation
- Proof-reading
- Note-taking
- Planning and writing memos, letters and reports
- Form-filling

Number work

- Accuracy and efficiency in basic figure work

Perception and orientation

- Keeping place on page of text
- Analysing complex visual material, for example graphs, maps, tables of figures
- Distinguishing left and right
- Mapping the physical environment

Emotions, work attitudes and interaction

- Confidence building
- Assertiveness training
- Dealing with stress
- Reducing frustration and anxiety
- Interacting with colleagues

REASONABLE ADJUSTMENTS

Examples of adjustments that your employer could make are given in Chapter 11 (pages 158–162). Not all of these may be relevant to your job, but you should study the list to see what might be useful, and think carefully if there could be other things not on the list that would be helpful to you. Then type out your own full list of suggestions and give it to your employer.

FUNDING FOR ASSESSMENT, TRAINING AND IT SUPPORT

Funds are available through the Access to Work scheme to cover workplace needs assessments, training costs and purchase of equipment. To make an application, you should telephone your local Access to Work Business Centre.

If you have already had a workplace needs assessment, it is important *to state this clearly on your application form.* Otherwise you may find that you are automatically referred for another workplace needs assessment with an occupational psychologist. Even if a second assessment is done, the Access funding belongs to you – the applicant – *and can be used to finance the recommendations made in your initial report.*

KEY TIPS

- Ask your employer to arrange an assessment and to adapt your job specifications and working conditions to your needs.
- Contact your local Access to Work Centre to request funding for training and IT support.

CHAPTER 11

DYSLEXIA: A QUICK GUIDE FOR EMPLOYERS

DYSLEXIA

Dyslexia is often regarded simply as a difficulty with reading and writing, but in fact literacy difficulties are no more than 'surface symptoms' of weaknesses in more basic cognitive abilities – that is, memory, phonology, visual tracking, perception, spatial awareness and motor skills. The literacy (and numeracy) difficulties associated with these deficits may be severe and obvious, or they may be more subtle, showing themselves in general slowness rather than inaccuracy in tasks involving written English. Intellectual and creative abilities are not impaired.

DYSPRAXIA

Deficits in two of the areas mentioned above – spatial awareness and motor skills – are sometimes grouped separately under the label 'dyspraxia'. If dyspraxic difficulties are severe, they may need to be treated separately from the dyslexic difficulties (by an occupational therapist, for example). While dyspraxic difficulties are often associated with dyslexic difficulties, the converse is not necessarily the case.

> In this chapter, for convenience, the term 'dyslexia'
> is used to comprehend both
> dyslexic and dyspraxic difficulties.

EMOTIONS

By the time a dyslexic person reaches adulthood he or she will probably have been struggling for many years with difficulties that may never have been recognised or understood. In such cases the original difficulties are likely to be bound up with a constellation of unpleasant, and perhaps debilitating, emotions: anger, confusion, embarrassment, anxiety, depression. Confidence and self-esteem will also be low.

WORKPLACE DIFFICULTIES

The dyslexic difficulties outlined above affect efficiency in many workplace tasks. Among the problems most often reported are:

- Following written and spoken instructions
- Remembering and recording telephone numbers and messages
- Spelling
- Inaccuracy in number work
- Note-taking
- Filing and looking up entries in directories
- Writing memos, letters and reports
- Form-filling
- Presentation of written work or figures
- Formulating thoughts rapidly enough to take part in discussions
- Keeping track of appointments and meetings
- Scheduling work and meeting deadlines

INTERACTION WITH COLLEAGUES

People with undiagnosed dyslexic difficulties are often a mystery not only to themselves, but also to those for whom, and with whom, they work. They may be withdrawn and seem unwilling to pull their weight, or they may appear to be oversensitive and aggressive. In general such employees are often difficult to 'place': they seem ambitious to progress in their career but are constantly hindered by inefficiency and a baffling inertia.

POSITIVE ASPECTS OF DYSLEXIC DIFFICULTIES

Dyslexic people who try to succeed in their work despite their difficulties know the meaning of hard work, long hours and determination. Further, the fact that they are not in the general mould of analytical thinking may mean that they develop other, more holistic ways of dealing with workplace tasks. Many dyslexics excel, for instance, in lateral thinking; they are creative and innovative, and are aware of links and associations that may escape the more linear thinker. They often have good powers of visualisation, excellent practical skills, and an untaught intuitive understanding of how systems work.

ASSESSMENT

Assessment should be carried out by a psychologist or dyslexia tutor *who specialises in assessing dyslexic difficulties in the workplace and providing consultancy to employers.* See pages 38–41 and 183–185 for advice on finding an assessor.

The assessment should include both a cognitive (diagnostic) assessment and a workplace needs assessment. The employer should receive a detailed assessment report in which the diagnostic and needs components of the assessment are clearly distinguished. In particular, the report should include the following:

Diagnostic assessment

- Detailed educational/occupational history
- Comprehensive assessment of general cognitive abilities
- Assessment and detailed analysis of literacy skills, including *timed* tests of reading and writing
- A consideration of emotional problems related to the dyslexic difficulties

Workplace needs assessment

- Analysis of the way in which the strengths and weaknesses identified in the diagnostic assessment relate to the employee's work performance
- Recommendations for an individual training programme tailored to the employee's needs
- Advice on IT support/technological aids that may be helpful
- Recommendations for adjustments that employers could make in workplace practice

TRAINING

Dyslexia tuition/training

It is crucially important to engage a tutor *who specialises in helping dyslexic adults who have workplace difficulties.* Few tutors have this specialty so it may require a certain amount of travelling for the employee to see an appropriate person. Training is found to be more effective if it is spread out over a period of months. This allows time for:

- Development of competence
- Trial of different strategies
- Practice in implementing new working methods
- Continuous feedback to the trainer

It is suggested that an initial programme of 40 hours' training be arranged; this could be on the basis of, say, a two- or three-hour session once a fortnight over a period of six months. The programme could then be extended, if thought desirable.

The training programme could include help with:

- Oral and listening skills
- Memory and concentration
- Visual tracking
- Work organisation and efficient work methods
- Reading and writing work documents
- Accuracy in number work
- Contributing to meetings
- Dealing with interviews
- Interaction with colleagues and clients
- Dealing with stress and anxiety

There are at present no major research studies investigating the effectiveness of dyslexia training in the workplace. However, there are many reports of single-case studies which show that motivated employees who are given appropriate training do significantly improve their skills.

The person who carries out the initial dyslexia assessment may also be able to offer training, or to recommend a suitable tutor. Please see pages 183–185 for other suggestions. It should be emphasised that the tuition needs of dyslexic adults are not usually met by short intensive-training courses, general adult literacy classes, or tuition by tutors whose practice is mainly with children.

IT support/technological aids

There is a wide range of hardware and software aids available for dyslexic people, and detailed advice is given on these on pages 173–180. Listed below are some of the most widely-used items:

- Mind-mapping software to facilitate planning and production of, for example, flow charts, reports and work schedules
- Voice recognition software to convert speech into text
- Text-to-speech software to read documents, files or web pages
- Pocket PC to help with work organisation
- Digital voice recorder with external microphone to record meetings and discussions
- Hand-held spell-checker/dictionary
- Talking calculator

It is important that any software or equipment you purchase is tailored to your employee's individual needs. It is, therefore, recommended that, before any purchases are made, you arrange a consultancy session with an expert who specialises in advising dyslexic people about IT support and technological aids. Such an expert may be found through the British Dyslexia Association, or see pages 187–188.

OPTOMETRY

Many dyslexic people suffer from an associated condition called visual stress. This means that they see letters 'jumping about on the page', and find that white paper 'glares'. In such a case it may be useful to arrange an assessment with an optometrist who specialises in colorimetry. The optometrist will advise on whether tinted lenses or some form of treatment would be useful. See pages 188–9 for advice on suitably qualified optometrists.

REASONABLE ADJUSTMENTS

Below are some suggestions for reasonable adjustments that can be made in the workplace to help and support dyslexic employees. The dyslexia trainer will be able to advise on which of these adjustments would be useful in a particular case, or to suggest other appropriate adjustments.

Dyslexia awareness

- Become informed about dyslexia and its effects, both practical and emotional
- Become informed about the related syndrome of dyspraxia, and its effects
- Remember that dyslexic employees will find written work and aspects of organisation much harder than most people, and will need to apply extra effort in many areas. This may make them prone to fatigue

- Encourage employees to talk to you and others about workplace difficulties, rather than conceal them
- Allow absence from work for dyslexia-specific training

Job applications

Application forms:
- Send by e-mail or disc if possible, so that the applicant can use a spell checker and easily revise what they have written
- If sending the form as hard copy, use a pastel-coloured paper to reduce visual stress

Interviews:
- Provide a copy of questions either during or before the interview; otherwise bear in mind that the applicant may need to have some questions repeated
- Be aware that the applicant may be somewhat slow in formulating answers to questions
- Be aware that his/her usual coping strategies may break down under the stress of an interview situation
- If the applicant becomes flustered or distressed, allow him/her a few minutes' break

Assessment tests:
- Read the test instructions out loud to the applicant, or present them on tape
- Allow the applicant to give his or her answers orally
- Allow more time than usual for the test to be completed
- If the requirements of the test do not reflect the requirements of the job, consider waiving the test

Verbal communication

- Give full, clear instructions, and take time to explain things properly
- Repeat things, if necessary. Check back understanding
- Give written or taped instructions as well as oral ones, as necessary

Written communication

Reading:
- Present written instructions in a clear format, if necessary in a flow chart
- Present information on audio or videotape as well as in writing
- Use voice mail rather than written memos
- Provide text-to-speech software
- Allow extra time for reading tasks

Writing:
- Provide speech-to-text software
- Allow extra time for writing tasks
- Do not expect the employee to take notes or dictation at speed

Work organisation

- Give advance notice of tasks whenever possible rather than setting sudden deadlines
- Offer help on planning and prioritising the workload and scheduling daily work tasks

- Encourage the employee to break down large tasks or projects into subsections and stages
- Offer guidance and support with new or difficult tasks
- Provide a wall planner that visually highlights appointments and deadlines

Reducing stress and anxiety

- Try not to put pressure on the employee by showing impatience or irritation
- Try not to interrupt the employee in mid-task
- Arrange particular times when the employee can work free from interruptions
- Provide non-stressful lighting (fluorescent lighting in particular can be troublesome for people who suffer from visual stress)
- If possible, provide a quiet, undisturbed workplace; alternatively, provide the employee with ear defenders
- Encourage the employee to take brief breaks, as this will increase overall output for the day

Training courses

- Be aware that reluctance to apply for promotion or training courses may be linked to fears of excessive paperwork and the possible exposure of weaknesses during training
- Ensure that in-house training courses have a *Good Practice* policy in relation to dyslexic trainees. For example, trainers should:

- o Provide a clear outline of their talks beforehand
- o Repeat things, if necessary
- o Leave a few minutes at the end of a session to check that dyslexic trainees have understood the main points made in the session
- o Write clearly on flipcharts
- o Be aware that whiteboard can cause visual stress

GENERAL CONSULTANCY

Some assessors/trainers offer a general consultancy service to employers who would like to raise awareness of dyslexia among their staff. See pages 183–184 for details of workplace consultancy organisations. The consultancy could take a variety of forms:

- A discussion with your team
- A talk to interested staff
- A seminar
- A training day

ACCESS TO WORK FUNDING

Funding for training and IT support is available through the Access to Work scheme. For details of this, contact your local Access to Work Business Centre. If your employee has had a diagnostic assessment, but not a workplace needs assessment, the latter can be arranged through Access to Work.

KEY TIP

- Photocopy this chapter and show it to your employer so that he or she can gain a better understanding of the nature of your difficulties.

CHAPTER 12

THE DISABILITY DISCRIMINATION ACT 1995 AND DYSLEXIA

If you have dyslexic and/or dyspraxic difficulties that are disabling to you in everyday life, then your employer is obliged, in accordance with the Disability Discrimination Act (1995), to make reasonable adjustments in the workplace to help you manage your difficulties. In this chapter the provisions of the Act are explained, and examples are given of employment tribunal cases.

WHAT THE ACT SAYS

According to Section 1(1) of the Act:
   'A person has a disability for the purposes of this Act if he has a *physical or mental impairment* which has a *substantial* and *long-term adverse effect* on his ability to carry out *normal day-to-day activities*.'

To judge whether you would be covered by the Act, you need to establish four things:

1. That your dyslexia is a mental impairment

The guidance to the Act specifically mentions dyslexia as an example of mental impairment, so this point is not likely to be disputed in court.

2. That your difficulties are substantial

This means that your difficulties are serious enough to be beyond the normal differences in ability that exist among people; in other words, they are more than minor or trivial.

In deciding whether a person's difficulties are beyond the normal range, the court will discount any artificial aids that may make the condition in question less serious. For example, for a person who wears a hearing aid, the effect of the hearing impairment is decided by reference to what the hearing level would be *without* the hearing aid.

It can be argued that the 'coping strategies' that dyslexic people use to manage their difficulties are in the same category as a hearing aid. You could lose your coping strategies in certain situations – for example, if you are under stress or have to work to a tight deadline. So the court needs to take into account the level of your difficulties when, for whatever reason, your coping strategies have broken down.

The following tribunal case illustrates this.

TRIBUNAL CASE 1

Mrs C was employed as a social worker at a residential facility for people with autism. Her written work was always good but this was due at least in part to the fact that she was very conscientious and often took work home. In other words, her coping strategy was to take extra care and time over her work. The tribunal, in finding that she was disabled, took account of (a) the fact that her coping mechanisms were likely to break down under stress, and (b) her employers had failed to take account of the fact that she was conscientious and worked extra hours in her own time.

3. Long-term effects

It is not usually in dispute that developmental dyslexia and dyspraxia have long-term effects, since these conditions will generally have been present from an early age, even if not identified until later in life.

4. Adverse effect on normal day-to-day activities

In the case of dyslexia, adverse effects would include problems with memory and the ability to concentrate, learn or understand. In the case of dyspraxia, there would also be problems with physical coordination. The guidance to the Act states that normal day-to-day activities are *not* intended to be job-specific: account should be taken of how far an activity is normal for most people on a frequent and fairly regular basis.

The day-to-day difficulties could include:

Reading letters, newspapers, official documents, recipes, safety/operating instructions on household gadgets, bus and train timetables, instructions on ticket and cash machines, entries in dictionaries and directories, signposts.

Writing cheques, messages, letters, shopping lists; filling in forms.

Checking bank statements; **keeping track** of outstanding bills.

Placing orders/conducting enquiries over the telephone.

Analysing complex visual material, such as maps; **finding way about** in unfamiliar surroundings.

Organising daily life: keeping track of appointments; remembering where things have been put.

Performing physical tasks: handwriting, cooking, dressing, driving.

The following two tribunal cases, in which different

decisions were given, illustrate the fact that the difficulties must be everyday ones, not simply work-related.

TRIBUNAL CASE 2

Mr J, who had dyslexia, worked for the Council as a residential social worker. His employers felt that, although he was dyslexic, he was not disabled within the meaning of the Act as there was no evidence that his difficulties were hindering his efficiency at work. However, the tribunal held it would be wrong to consider normal day-to-day activities only in the context of Mr J's job. Many ordinary, day-to-day tasks such as shopping, banking and reading simple instructions require literacy skills and, since Mr J had a difficulty with such tasks that was more than trivial, he was disabled for the purposes of the Act.

TRIBUNAL CASE 3

By contrast, in the case of Miss R an opposite judgement was given. Miss R's job involved sorting information records into sequence and her employers became aware that she made a high number of errors. The tribunal found that, although Miss R was dyslexic, she did not experience any day-to-day problems other than in her job, where spelling was a particular problem. She was not therefore entitled to the protection of the Act and the employer was not obliged to make reasonable adjustments.

(Source for case reports: IDS Brief 682.)

HOW TO USE THE ACT

It may well be the case that, if you make your difficulties known to your employer, the latter will be prepared to arrange an assessment and a course of training for you, and to make appropriate adjustments in the workplace. If, however, you feel that your employer is treating you unfairly or not providing adequate support, you could take your case to an employment tribunal.

To succeed in your claim, you would need first to establish that your difficulties constitute a disability, and then show that you have been less favourably treated by your employer because of your disability, or that your employer has failed to make reasonable adjustments.

In making your claim, you could seek the support of your union, or one of the disability or legal organisations listed on page 190.

The Act can be read online at: www.opsi.gov.uk

KEY TIPS

- The Disability Discrimination Act 1995 includes provisions covering dyslexia and dyspraxia in the workplace.
- Studying those parts of the Act that might apply to you can help you understand your rights at work and your employer's responsibilities towards you.

EPILOGUE

I hope that you have enjoyed this book and found it helpful. If, having reached the end of it, you seem to have forgotten most of what you've read, don't worry: this happens to a lot of people, and to dyslexic people more than most. The best thing is to try to take on board all the information *gradually*. Read again through the chapters, especially those in Part B on improving skills. Give yourself a week to read each chapter carefully and to practise the work strategies suggested in it. Discuss these, if possible, with family, friends and colleagues. And finally, don't forget the advice given throughout the book about being assertive: you have a right to take up your own space in this world, and to put into it both your difficulties and your talents.

I know that all the people mentioned in this book will join me in wishing you success in the future.

Dr Sylvia Moody

USEFUL EQUIPMENT

In this section you will find *general* information on IT and technological support for people with dyslexic difficulties. For advice on *specific* items of hardware or software packages that would suit your particular requirements, consult a specialist in the field (see pages 187–188). Try to get a hands-on demonstration or a free trial of software before purchasing anything. Note that price is not always an indicator of usefulness.

You may be able to apply for VAT relief on certain items. For advice on this contact iANSYST Ltd: 0800 018 0045 or reception@dyslexic.com

ORGANISATION

Pocket PCs (PPCs) are hand-sized organisers that work like mini-computers. They can store your diary, set alarmed reminders for appointments, create 'to-do' lists, store pictures, record notes and messages, and store documents for reading and editing wherever you are. You can synchronise your PPC with your desktop PC or laptop to keep your diary and contacts list up to date.

Caution: The battery life on PPCs can be quite limited. If the battery is not kept charged, you could lose all the information you have stored.

If you don't have a PPC, there are some useful tools available within Microsoft Office, which are often pre-installed on your computer. Microsoft Outlook, for example, has a simple-to-use calendar/diary function with audible alarm.

SPEECH RECOGNITION

There are software packages that allow you to dictate into your computer and have the written word appear on the screen. The text can then be edited and printed, using, for example, Microsoft Word. The software also has the ability to 'transcribe' voice recordings from digital recorders and PPCs.

Caution: Speech-recognition software is trained to understand *your* voice, so it will *not* be able to transcribe recordings of talks and meetings.

TEXT-TO-SPEECH

Text-to-speech programs can read out loud practically any text that is on the screen. Hearing what you have written read back to you often helps with proofing your work.

SCANNING

Optical character recognition (OCR) software can scan printed documents and convert them into text documents on your computer. You can then read the documents on your computer screen in the colour and format that suits you best: perhaps in larger print, with double spacing, or using different-coloured backgrounds and print. Or use text-to-speech software to have the documents read aloud to you.

Caution: Scanning whole books or large amounts of text is laborious and usually not worth the effort.

NOTE-TAKING

You can use a digital voice recorder to 'jot down' notes and reminders to yourself, which can then be played back or transcribed into a text document on your computer using speech-recognition software. The recorder can also be used to record talks and meetings for playing back at a later time, reducing the need to take hand-written notes.

Recording efficiency varies according to the acoustic environment. It is usually preferable to use an external microphone.

Caution: Make sure you choose a recorder that has a long recording time and PC connectivity.

TYPING TUTORS

Being able to type confidently, accurately and quickly will free your mind up to concentrate on the content of what you are typing. There are several computer-interactive typing tutors that will give you training in touch-typing.

SPELLING

Make sure you are making the best use of the spell-checkers that come as standard within, for example, Microsoft Office. There are also sophisticated add-ons to word-processing packages that offer phonetic and homophone spell-checkers, and word prediction. Hand-held spell-checkers are also available.

PLANNING WRITTEN WORK

You can plan and structure reports and other documents using computer-generated 'spider maps' and flow charts. At the click of your mouse these maps can be converted into text and exported to your preferred word-processing package, presentation software (such as Powerpoint), or other software packages. You can then edit the text using the keyboard or voice-recognition software, and finally proof it with the help of a screen reader.

GIVING TALKS / PRESENTATIONS

Check if your employer can provide an 'interactive' whiteboard, linked to a computer. You can then:

- Write on the screen to highlight and annotate points in documents and presentations
- View and navigate the Internet and display websites that your whole audience will be able to see
- Project movie files and DVDs onto a large screen
- Allow members of the audience to add their contributions to word-processing documents, spreadsheets, and so on, by writing directly onto them
- Save information for printing as handout notes, or uploading onto the Internet/Intranet

Whiteboard 'glare' can be avoided by changing the colours projected onto the screen through the computer's Windows properties/appearance function.

COLOUR-SENSITIVITY

Microsoft Windows operating systems allow customisation of your computer with tools designed to help users with disabilities. For example, changing screen and font colours can reduce eye strain and prevent text from 'swimming' on the page. These functions are, however, limited, and you may prefer to buy a specialised piece of software that can change all Windows colours, including the background colour, default text colour, menu background, text colour and toolbars. Similar software for web pages is also available.

When reading books or papers, you could use coloured overlays or reading rulers to stabilise the words. Professional overlays are available from Cerium Visual Technologies; and eye-level coloured reading rulers are available from Crossbow Education (see pages 188, 189).

SCREEN RULERS

If you have difficulty keeping your place on the screen, a screen ruler could be helpful. Acting as an 'overlay' on the screen, it creates a ruler that can be moved up and down with the mouse. Some versions can dim out areas of the screen that are not in use.

ROUTE PLANNING AND NAVIGATION SYSTEMS

Route planners are computer programs displaying street maps and road networks throughout the UK and abroad. They enable you to plot the route to your destination, and can be accessed through a website, your desktop PC, laptop, or PPC. Some systems let you print out maps of the proposed route as well as directions, such as when to take a turn.

Navigation aids are linked to the global positioning system (GPS), which uses satellites to locate your position anywhere in the world to within a few metres. The software can direct you along a route as you travel.

Caution: Take care to choose the style of interface that suits you best. Some people prefer detailed maps, others simple directional arrows.

PORTABLE DATA STORAGE

You can copy your files onto a USB storage device (not much larger than your thumb) and carry them around with you. To access your data, simply plug the device into another PC.

GOOD WORKING PRACTICES

Choose a chair that supports your back; don't slump on a couch or work with a laptop on your knee.

Don't sit too close to the screen. If possible, have the screen at right angles to the light source.

If you find that working on a laptop causes strain or discomfort, consider buying an external full-sized keyboard and mouse. An ergonomic keyboard (designed for comfort and ease of use) is a wise investment as it encourages good posture. Dyspraxic people, in particular, find this type of keyboard helpful. Also useful: wrist rests, and mouse pads with wrist support.

BUYING HARDWARE AND SOFTWARE – GENERAL ADVICE

If you already own a computer, don't purchase any software until you've checked with the supplier that it is compatible with your equipment.

When considering purchasing a new computer, think carefully before choosing between a laptop and a desktop PC. Laptops are easy to carry around, but they are easily damaged or stolen. They can also cost considerably more than a desktop PC.

Specialist software is not widely available in high street stores, but it can usually be purchased over the Internet. Before buying anything, get up-to-date advice on all your hardware and software requirements.

USEFUL ADDRESSES

HELP AND ADVICE ORGANISATIONS

Bangor Dyslexia Unit
University of Wales, Gwynedd LL57 2DG
Tel: 01248 382 203
E-mail: dyslex-admin@bangor.ac.uk
Website: www.dyslexia.bangor.ac.uk
This branch covers the whole of Wales.

British Dyslexia Association (BDA)
98 London Road, Reading, Berks RG1 5AU
Tel: 01189 668 271
E-mail: helpline@bdadyslexia.org.uk
Website: www.bdadyslexia.org.uk
For list of all local associations, click on Information.

Dyslexia Association of Ireland
1 Suffolk Street, Dublin 2
Tel: 01 679 0276
E-mail: info@dyslexia-ie
Website: www.dyslexia.ie

Dyslexia Association of London
Dyslexia Resource Centre, The Munro Centre,
  66 Snowsfields, London SE1 3SS
Tel: 020 7407 0900
E-mail: dal1449@btconnect.com
Website: www.dyslexiainlondon.ik.com

Dyslexia in Scotland
Stirling Business Centre, Wellgreen, Stirling FK8 2DZ
Tel: 01786 446650
E-mail: info@dyslexia-in-scotland.org
Website: www.dyslexia.scotland.dial.pipex.com

Dyslexia Parents Resource
Website: www.dyslexia-parent.com
Gives contact details for all BDA local associations.

European Dyslexia Association
E-mail: eda@kbnet.co.uk
Website: www.dyslexia.eu.com

International Dyslexia Association
Website: www.interdys.org

DYSLEXIA ASSESSMENT AND TUITION

It is important that assessment and tuition are carried out by chartered psychologists or tutors who are dyslexia specialists and have experience in working with adults. Consult your local branch of the British Dyslexia Association (see page 181) or Dyslexia Action (see page 184) for advice.

Workplace dyslexia specialists:

Adult Dyslexia and Skills Development Centre
1–7 Woburn Walk, London WC1H 0SS
Tel: 020 7388 8744
E-mail: dyslexia@adsdc.freeserve.co.uk

Dyslexia Advice and Training Services
33 South Grove House, South Grove, London N6 6LR
Tel: 020 348 7110
E-mail: brianhagan2003@yahoo.co.uk

Dyslexia Assessment and Consultancy
39 Cardigan Street, Kennington, London SE11 5PF
Tel: 020 8090 2298
Fax: 020 7587 0546
E-mail: info@workingwithdyslexia.com
Website: www.workingwithdyslexia.com

Dyslexia Assessment Service
22 Wray Crescent, London N4 3LP
Tel: 020 7272 6429

Dyslexia Consultancy
6 Gilbert Road, Malvern, Worcs WR14 3RQ
Tel: 01684 572 466
E-mail: dyslexia.mj@dsl.pipex.com

Fitzgibbon Associates
39-41 North Road, London N7 9DP
Tel: 020 7609 7809
E-mail: fae@fitzgibbonassociates.co.uk

Key4Learning
The Old Village Stores, Cheap Street, Chedworth, Gloucester GL54 4AA
Tel: 01285 720 964
E-mail: enquiries@key4learning.com
Website: www.key4learning

Workplace needs assessment only:

Access to Work Business Centres
Contact directory enquiries for local Centre, or ask at your local JobCentrePlus.

General assessment and tuition for Adults:

Dyslexia Action
Park House, Wick Road, Egham, Surrey TW20 0HH
Tel: 01784 222 300
E-mail: info@dyslexiaaction.org.uk
Website: www.dyslexiaaction.org.uk

Dyslexia Teaching Centre
23 Kensington Square, London W8 5HN
Tel: 020 7361 4790
E-mail: dyslexiateacher@tiscali.co.uk
Website: www.dyslexia-teaching-centre.org.uk

Helen Arkell Dyslexia Centre
Frensham, Farnham, Surrey GU10 3BW
Tel: 01252 792 400
E-mail: enquiries@arkellcentre.org.uk
Website: www.arkellcentre.org.uk
Covers Surrey, Hampshire, Southwest London.

London Dyslexia Action
2 Grosvenor Gardens, London SW1W 0DH
Tel: 020 7730 8890
E-mail: london@dyslexiaaction.org.uk
Website: www.dyslexiaaction.org.uk

PATOSS (dyslexia tutors organisation)
PO Box 10, Evesham, Worcestershire WR11 6ZW
Tel: 01386 712650
E-mail: patoss@evesham.ac.uk
Website: www.patoss-dyslexia.org

Tuition for Dyslexic Adults
20a Pymmes Green Road, London N11 1BY
Tel: 020 8368 3634
E-mail: dianabart@aol.com

DYSPRAXIA SUPPORT

Developmental Adult Neuro-Diversity Association (DANDA)
46 Westbere Road, London NW2 3RU
Tel: 020 7435 7891
E-mail: mary@pmcolley.freeserve.co.uk
Website: www.danda.org.uk

Dyscovery Centre
4a Church Road, Whitchurch, Cardiff CF14 2DZ
Tel: 02920 628 222
E-mail: info@dyscovery.co.uk
Website: www.dyscovery.co.uk

Dyspraxia Association of Ireland
69a Main Street, Leixlip, Co Kildare
Tel: 01 295 7125
E-mail: info@dyspraxiaireland.com
Website: www.dyspraxiaireland.com

Dyspraxia Foundation
8 West Alley, Hitchin, Herts SG5 1EG
Tel: 01462 455 016
E-mail: admin@dyspraxiafoundation.org.uk
Website: www.dyspraxiafoundation.org.uk

Dyspraxia Connexion
21 Birchdale Avenue, Hucknall, Notts NG15 6DL
Tel: 0115 963 2220
Website: www.dysf.fsnet.co.uk

WORKPLACE ADVICE

Dyslexia Adults link
Website: www.dyslexia-adults.com
Offers general advice for adult dyslexics and has an
extensive section on workplace difficulties.

JobCentrePlus
Website: www.jobcentreplus.gov.uk/cms.asp
Offers advice on coping with disability in the workplace.

IT ADVICE AND TRAINING

AbilityNet
PO Box 94, Warwick CV34 5WS
Tel: 01926 312847 or 0800 269545 (helpline freephone)
E-mail: enquiries@abilitynet.org.uk
Website: www.abilitynet.org.uk

Dyslexia in the Workplace
Flat 2, Grafton Chambers, Churchway, London NW1 1LN
Tel: 020 7388 3807
E-mail: workplacedyslexia@btopenworld.com

Iansyst Training Project
Fen House, Fen Road, Cambridge CB4 1UN
Tel: 01223 420101
E-mail: reception@dyslexic.com
Website: www.dyslexic.com

To find a local consultant, check with your local branch of the British Dyslexia Association (see page 181).

VISUAL PROBLEMS

Colorimetry assessment

Colorimetry assessments are not done in standard eye tests; contact the Dyslexia Research Trust or Cerium Visual Technologies (below) for a specialist in your area.

Barnard Associates
58 Clifton Gardens, London NW11 7EL
Tel: 020 8458 0599
E-mail: simon@eye-spy.co.uk

Cerium Visual Technologies
Tenterden, Kent TN30 7DE
Tel: 01580 765 211
E-mail: ceriumuk@ceriumvistech.co.uk
Website: www.ceriumvistech.co.uk
Sells tinted overlays.

Crossbow Education
41 Sawpit Lane, Brocton, Stafford ST17 0TE
Tel: 01785 660902
E-mail: sales@crossboweducation.com
Website: www.crossboweducation.com
Sells eye-level coloured reading rulers.

Dyslexia Research Trust
University Laboratory of Physiology, Oxford OX1 3PT
Tel: 01865 272 116
Website: www.dyslexic.org.uk

Institute of Optometry
56–62 Newington Causeway, London SE1 6DS
Tel: 020 7234 9641
E-mail: admin@ioo.org.uk
Website: www.ioo.org.uk

LISTENING BOOKS

Among the audio libraries that offer a mail-order service
are:

Calibre
Website: www.calibre.org.uk

Listening Books
Website: www.listening-books.org.uk

LEGAL ADVICE

Disability Rights Commission
Tel: 08457 622 633
Website: www.drc-gb.org

Legal Services Commission
Websites: www.legalservices.gov.uk
www.clsdirect.org.uk

Law Centres
Website: www.lawcentres.org.uk

Disability Law Service
Website: www.dls.org.uk

Office of Public Sector Information
Website: www.opsi.gov.uk
Type 'Disability Discrimination Act' into the 'search'
window to read the relevant sections of the Act in full.

GENERAL COUNSELLING

British Association of Counselling
35–37 Albert Street, Rugby, Warwickshire CV21 2SG
Tel: 0870 443 5252
E-mail: bacp@bacp.co.uk
Website: www.bacp.co.uk

GP surgeries sometimes have counsellors. Also your
local **Council** or **radio helpdesk** may have details of
local counselling organisations.

FURTHER AND HIGHER EDUCATION

SKILL: National Bureau for Students with Disabilities
Chapter House, 18–20 Crucifix Lane, London SEI 3JW
Tel: 020 7450 0620
E-mail: skill@skill.org.uk
Website: www.skill.org.uk

World of Dyslexia Ltd
Website: www.dyslexia-college.com
Offers useful information on topics from reading
techniques to applying for grants.

FURTHER READING

GENERAL INTEREST

The Adult Dyslexic: Interventions and Outcomes, David McLoughlin, Carol Leather and Patricia Stringer (Whurr Publishers, 1999)

Dyslexia and Stress, Tim Miles (ed.) (Whurr Publishers, 2004)

The Dyslexic Adult in a Non-dyslexic World, Ellen Morgan and Cynthia Klein (Whurr Publishers, 2000)

Making Dyslexia Work for You: A Self-help Guide, Vicki Goodwin and Bonita Thomson (David Fulton Publishers, 2004)

FOR PEOPLE IN EMPLOYMENT

Dyslexia in the Workplace, Diana Bartlett and Sylvia Moody (Whurr Publishers, 2000)

Dyslexia in Adults: Education and Employment, Gavin Reid and Jane Kirk (John Wiley, 2001)

Adult Dyslexia: a Guide for the Workplace, Gary Fitzgibbon and Brian O'Connor (John Wiley, 2002)

FOR EMPLOYERS

Briefing Paper 6 on Dyslexia in the Workplace, available from Employers Forum on Disability (Tel: 020 7403 3020; www.employers-forum.co.uk)

FOR UNIONS

Dyslexia in the Workplace: a Guide for Unions, Brian Hagan (available from the TUC)

FOR STUDENTS

Dyslexia at College, Tim Miles and Dorothy Gilroy (Routledge, 1995)
Dyslexia: a Teenager's Guide, Sylvia Moody (Vermilion, 2004)
Use Your Head, Tony Buzan (BBC Active, 2003)

FOR TEACHERS

Dyslexia in Secondary School: A Practical Handbook for Teachers, Parents and Students, Jenny Cogan and Mary Flecker (Whurr Publishers, 2004)
Dyslexia and the Curriculum – a series of books covering individual GCSE subjects (British Dyslexia Association/David Fulton)

DYSPRAXIA

Living with Dyspraxia, Mary Colley (ed.) (Dyspraxia
    Foundation, 2000)

Index

ALSO AVAILABLE FROM VERMILION
BY DR SYLVIA MOODY

☐ Dyslexia: A Teenager's Guide   9780091900014   £8.99

FREE POSTAGE AND PACKING
Overseas customers allow £2.00 per paperback

ORDER:

By phone: 01624 677237

By post: Random House Books
c/o Bookpost
PO Box 29
Douglas
Isle of Man IM991BQ

By fax: 01624 670923

By email: bookshop@enterprise.net

Cheques (payable to Bookpost)
and credit cards accepted

Prices and availability subject to change without notice.
Allow 28 days for delivery.
When placing your order, please mention if you do not wish to
receive any additional information.

www.randomhouse.co.uk